YOU SIMPLY CAN'T TRUST A TALKING BIRD

And Other Stories That Will Warm Your Heart

BY WALTER ALBRITTON

Fairway Press
Lima, Ohio

YOU SIMPLY CAN'T TRUST A TALKING BIRD

FIRST EDITION

7931 / ISBN 1-55673-481-6 PRINTED IN U.S.A.

Dedicated to
the many friends in our community
whose encouragement has kept me writing

Table Of Contents

Introduction

I am indebted to my friend, Ann Cipperly, for motivating me to write the material contained in this book. At the time Ann was serving as editor of the "Living Section" of *The Opelika-Auburn News*, a daily newspaper serving our community.

I was hesitant to take Ann up on her invitation: to write a regular Sunday column for her "Living Section," a column which would run alongside "Dear Abby" and the wedding announcements. Ann also wrote regular feature articles about exotic dishes she had sampled at famous restaurants and exciting vacation spots she and her husband Don had visited.

Tossing the writings of a preacher into this mix did not seem like a great idea to me. Perhaps it was my pride that made me balk. After all, I thought, I would prefer to have my column run on the editorial page beside the sage advice of Lewis Grizzard, James Kilpatrick, and the like. But no, Ann wanted my column to appear with the recipes and the engagement announcements!

And just what was she looking for? If it was a syrupy, turn your heart toward God sermonette, then I was not interested. "Not at all," she said. "Write about life from your perspective; after all, this is the 'Living' Section!" So we agreed that I would share ideas about life, but without sounding too much like a preacher. This was my own idea. I felt that people would not be interested in one more mini-sermon.

But loving intrigue I decided to name the column "Altar Call," which would create the impression that my articles were the sermonizings of a preacher pleading for converts. That, however, I would try to avoid, in the hope that I might reach persons who were indifferent toward, or estranged from, the Church.

So in these little essays I have addressed a variety of subjects, offering perspectives about life which hopefully will cause the reader to see that the Author of life wants people to enjoy living and to live life to the fullest. No life is well lived that is not laced with laughter.

The preacher people see and hear in the pulpit every Sunday is not always the real person. In these articles, dear reader, you will find windows into the mind and heart of one preacher who wants very much to be real. And being real for me is seeing the funny side of the commonplace, and having a good laugh, often at my own expense. Like you, I am made in the image of God. And if God does not have a sense of humor, then I have not learned anything during my 60 years in this world.

We shall all suffer, and we shall all die. But if we are wise, before we die we may choose to enjoy life!

You Simply Can't Trust A Talking Bird

Preachers usually have to learn things the way most people do, the hard way. We may study hard and win our credentials, but we are still wet behind the ears when we begin pastoral work.

No amount of study or degrees will make a person an effective preacher. Like everybody else, we get our real education through on the job training.

If we are lucky we soon learn that book learning is not nearly as important as good old horse sense. People will not begin to care about what you know until they know you care about them as persons.

One of the first traps a preacher can fall into is believing that folks really want to know his plan for building up the church. I learned that the hard way.

In my first appointment some of my church leaders invited me to tell them my program for making the church hum, and assured me they were ready to follow me to hell and back. So I called on my special training as a seminary graduate and laid out a plan for the church. It fizzled faster than a pat of butter in July sunshine.

There is not the slightest chance under heaven that folks are ready to follow the plan of their new preacher as soon as he takes over the pulpit. What they really want to hear when they ask him for his program is something like this: "I really don't have a plan. You folks have been here serving God for years, and I want to learn from you what works best in this situation. You have done a great work for God here for a long time, and I need your help."

Those are only words, of course, and words alone are not very convincing. Before you can lead, you must follow, learn, and care. People are really listening more for the beat of your heart than the sound of your voice.

They want to know if you really care about the hurts and heartaches of their lives. They want to know if you believe in them, and if you are willing to walk where they walk, and hurt where they hurt, until you understand some of their deepest disappointments and the longings of their hearts.

Then, and only then, will they begin to give you the privilege of leadership. The preacher is a fool who takes for granted that he will have authority because of his position or his training. People will follow you only when they have witnessed your own blood, sweat, and tears as you have lived in the trenches with them.

So most of us preachers have given up on importing some dandy little program to generate new life into our churches. We try to find out what the people believe will work for them, and we do this by visiting our folks where they live and work.

But even in the seemingly harmless activity of visiting people in their homes, we find that there are hard lessons to be learned. A generation ago, folks were disappointed if you called to make an appointment to visit them.

Back then folks were delighted when the preacher would pop in, and even more if he had time to take pot luck and eat with the family. Nowadays, people are likely to be a little irritated if you don't call ahead and come at a convenient time.

Pop calling can put you in an embarrassing situation sometimes. I can recall a few times when I wish I had stayed at home. Like the time the husband was not home but the wife, still in her night gown, insisted that I come in for a cup of coffee. She may have needed a lot of counseling, but I didn't stay long enough to find out.

My friend, Jim, learned a good lesson at one home a few years back. When he knocked on the door, he realized that it was open, so he stuck his head in and called out, "Anybody home?" A voice from within answered, "Come in, come in."

So Jim walked in, but almost had a heart attack when a huge Doberman pinscher suddenly pinned him against the wall, snarling angrily in his face. Desperately Jim glanced around the room, hoping the owner would call off his dog.

Unfortunately there was no one home, but there by the window was a cage with a bird inside that kept saying, "Come in, come in." Jim was frozen against the wall, sweating and praying. Realizing that no help was forthcoming, he yelled angrily at the bird, "You stupid bird, can't you say anything besides 'come in'!"

Whereupon the bird replied, "Sic him, sic him!"

That cured Jim of not calling ahead.

All of which goes to prove that, while there are a lot of folks preachers can't trust, they sure as heck can't trust a talking bird.

As far as I'm concerned, folks who insist on owning both a Doberman and a talking bird would probably be happier in the Presbyterian Church.

Watching Butterflies In The Rain

I get hungry and feel guilty every time I read one of my friend Ann Cipperly's columns about great places to visit. She makes my mouth water describing these wonderful restaurants and quaint show places, all of which my wife would love to see.

You see, I am a plodder. I get absorbed in my work. I have tunnel vision. People like me miss a lot of things that other people see. Not that we like that about ourselves, and we do try to improve.

For years I have been trying to spot a beautiful bird or a lovely flower before my wife does. But most of the time she sees it first, and points it out to me. While I respond with appropriate admiration for bird or flower, I am inwardly wanting to kick myself for not having seen it first!

But, back to the guilt. Plodders like me usually get dragged handcuffed to see lovely places and take the time to smell the roses. We are so busy. And, frankly, we just can't bring ourselves to believe that real men should ever stop working for no better reason than to drive somewhere, eat and look at flowers.

So, in an honest effort to improve, last Wednesday I gave in to the pestering notion that I should take Dean and her mom to see the butterflies at Callaway Gardens. Not that I needed to see them, mind you, but I knew they would enjoy getting out. Plus it would earn me some brownie points for being so thoughtful.

It was about 11:30 a.m. when I thought of going. Quickly I calculated the time needed, and concluded that we could leave at 2:30 p.m., arrive in time to see the butterflies, eat supper at the quaint little place on the hill, and be back in time for my 7:15 p.m. meeting. It was perfect! They would love it, and think I was wonderful.

When I called to spring my great plan on Dean, she dropped the phone, fainting when I told her my plan, but recovered quickly, and joyfully replied, "We'll be ready!" I was beaming with pride; my plan was working.

As we drove away from home at 2:35 p.m., my glorious plan began to unravel. The dark clouds overhead began releasing a furious rain as the bottom fell out. None of us said a word. But we were all thinking, "Walter really knows how to pick a day to go see the butterflies!"

My next stop was to get some money at the automatic teller window; it was not working, "temporarily closed for repair." So back home to pick up a check, and get it cashed, getting wet in the downpour. Umbrella? Of course not. Only a pessimist would have had an umbrella on hand.

By now I was soaked but still determined to go. I turned onto Interstate 85 at 3:10, into the face of blinding rain. I could hardly see 100 feet in front of me, but come hell or high water we were going to see those butterflies!

I consoled myself by figuring it might not be raining at the Gardens, but I was wrong. As we turned in the main gate the rain still peppering down, it suddenly dawned on me that it was not 4 p.m. at the Gardens; it was 5 p.m.! It was only an hour until the restaurant on the hill would close.

I tried not to choke upon learning the tickets cost me $21 when I had guessed they would be only $12 to $15. After all, Dean's mother is 92; shouldn't she be admitted for half fare, just for having lived so long?

Since we were pressed for time, I just knew the butterfly building would be right inside the gate. But no, you have to drive through half of Georgia to get to it. Finally we found it, but had to park 100 yards away because the parking area is being remodeled. Dean's mom walks at a snail's pace; need I say more? And it was uphill all the way.

As patiently as possible we pulled mom along, praying that she would not get soaked and come down with pneumonia. At last we made it to the famous home of the butterflies. Thank God I did not say it, but I think my wife guessed anyway that

I was thinking, "Hurry now, enjoy these butterflies quickly, so we can go!"

I had seen thousands of butterflies over the years — mostly on my car windshield. But at Callaway they are more beautiful than I had imagined, yet few were flying around. They were sitting on limbs and leaves, resting. Then I noticed a sign saying that butterflies are more active in the sunshine.

I walked on, hoping Dean would not notice that sign. She saw it, and as she was reading it, the rain began pouring down, pounding the domed ceiling above the butterflies. I knew she was thinking, "Yes, Walter really knows how to plan a trip."

On the way back to the car, downhill, Dean's mother became dizzy, and a stranger, who happened to be a nurse, had to assist her to the car. I easily read her mind: "Boy, are we having fun!"

The little restaurant closed as we drove up, so frantically I looked for another place to eat. With not too many choices, we agreed on one that seemed popular and took our places at a table. Fifteen minutes later a waitress yelled as she walked by, "Be with you in a minute, folks." Fifty minutes later our food arrived. Spaghetti, but no bread. I fumed, and finally got the bread as we finished the meal.

I really don't care that much for spaghetti, but the "Great Planner" had neglected to bring enough money, and I was sweating out the bill drinking water instead of tea. I made it, with 12 cents left after leaving a tip begrudgingly.

On the way back to Opelika I broke the speed limit as often as I dared, determined to get back in time for my committee meeting. By the grace of God I made it, deposited Dean and her mom at home, and made it to the church by 7:15.

Hurrying breathlessly into the church, proud that I had made it, I was greeted by my friend Janet who said, "Brother Walter, we tried all afternoon to call you to let you know our meeting has been canceled."

Fortunately Dean and her mom saw some humor in this hectic afternoon that I had arranged. And I did assuage my guilt for awhile. But please, don't mention butterflies to me anytime soon. The next one that flies by me had better be moving fast or it will be in the centerfold of my new collection!

Preachers Cry Like The Rest Of Us

After reading one of my recent Altar Call columns, a woman in our church said to me, "You're just like one of us; you hurt and cry just like we do."

It really felt good to hear her say that. She was able to identify with me. It helps us all to know that we are not alone in this world, that other people have many of the same struggles that we do.

All of us, for example, need affirmation. I don't mind admitting that I need it; I soak it up like a sponge. When someone expresses appreciation to me for something I have done, it feels good; it reinforces my sense of self-worth.

I make it a practice to enjoy my affirmations because I know I will get my share of criticism as well, and a lot of it is well deserved. I admit I don't enjoy criticism, but we all need that too. We may learn from our critics, and we may have the good fortune to win some of them as friends if we will accept their criticism gracefully.

One woman said she likes my preaching because it is so down to earth. I like that because it tells me she sees the connection I am trying to make between the gospel and real life. If faith does not help us with the practical problems of everyday life, then it is phony and useless. Deliver me from preaching that is too "heavenly" to be of any earthly use!

Preaching is dangerous business. When you preach one sermon to 100 people, you have really preached 100 different sermons because each person receives it through his/her own set of filters. Each person's experiences flavor, and sometimes distort what is heard.

How a person feels physically or emotionally also influences what is heard. If you have indigestion, or your back hurts, or you have had a spat with your spouse, you will hear a sermon through some very negative filters. On such a Sunday you may hear something the preacher did not really say, giving his words a meaning he did not intend for them to have.

But that is one of the risks preachers have to take — being misunderstood. We have to learn to take that in stride, and rejoice that now and then someone does understand, and decides to respond to God in such a way that a life is changed — not by the sermon but by the grace of God.

Some folks don't really want a preacher who is "like us." They want someone upon a pedestal, someone they can admire for his holier life. This idea perpetuates the erroneous principle of a double standard; one standard for clergy, another for laity. If they can believe this, then it gives them an excuse for "low" living. They can say, "God expects more from the clergy, but he understands that folks like us are human and subject to the ordinary frailties of the race."

Well, friends, I wasn't born on Mars and deposited in Elmore County by some alien space ship. And this double standard idea is a lie. God expects holiness from all of us! There is nothing in the Bible that says you are off the hook because you haven't been called to preach.

One Sunday years ago I shared my broken heart with my congregation. A woman said to me afterward, "How disappointing to learn that my preacher has the same problems we do!" I guess she wanted some spiritual angelic being for a pastor, someone who does not bleed, cry and hurt like the rest of the human race.

How I wish she had said, "How comforting, pastor, to know that you hurt like we do, and yet you are hanging in there, expecting help from our Lord. I got this help when I needed it, and I know you will too. I'll be praying for you."

In another church I wept one Sunday while preaching about how much it hurt to see our son suffer and die at age three. It was spontaneous; I didn't have "cry here" anywhere in my sermon notes.

After the service a man in his mid-sixties came up to me and embraced me with a bear hug. With tears in his own eyes he said, "You are one of us now; we know you cry like we do.'' I was so deeply moved I could not respond, except to embrace him again.

Three years later his oldest son had surgery. The doctor discovered cancer. I was with that man and his wife when the doctor shared the dreaded news, ''There is nothing we can do for your son.'' There in that little room we wept together again, and reached out to God for help. How thankful I was for the bonding that had already occured between my heart and his, so that I could share in his awful moment of anguish.

Perhaps the point is very simple. When you see your pastor as ''one of us,'' when you allow him to share the joys and sorrows of your life, when you laugh with him and cry with him, then you can really hear what he is trying to say on Sunday.

As long as he is just a professional performing in the pulpit, and you are just an observer in the pew, listening with a critical ear, nothing of lasting value is happening.

Maybe it takes pain and tears for us truly to know each other and to move from casual to creative relationships in which God is also known.

Even Preachers Have Fun

Preachers don't get invited to many parties, but God provides us with more fun than we can stand anyway. Weddings, for example, have always been a great source of entertainment for me.

Since most weddings are on our turf, I always go over the ground rules with the bride and groom. One rule is: No pictures are to be taken during the ceremony. A wedding after all is a service of worship. But on one occasion as I began to question the bride during the ceremony, someone near the front stood up and began snapping pictures like crazy. It was the bride's mother!

She got some good pictures, but she and her little flash bulbs also got about as much attention as the bride.

On another occasion I had a small wedding in the chapel with about 25 family members and friends present. It seemed like a routine affair though the groom was a bit nervous. I began with my usual charge to the couple about the sacredness of marriage. Then as I turned to the groom and asked him the question, "Will you have this woman to be your wedded wife?" he looked down at the floor and started shaking his head as if to say, "No, I can't do it."

Undaunted I charged on with my questions: "Will you love her, comfort her, honor and keep her, in sickness and in health; and forsaking all other keep thee only unto her, so long as you both shall live?" But suddenly — I think it was when I got to the "forsaking all other" line — he bolted and ran out of the chapel.

I stood there speechless, not knowing what to do or to say next. After a couple of minutes it was obvious the young man was not coming back. The embarrassed bride look helplessly at me and blurted out, "Do you think I should go after him?" I replied, "I wouldn't if I were you!"

Turning to the small crowd sitting in the chapel, I said, "Folks, I think this is our cue to leave; I'm going home." I felt sorry for the bride, but after all it may have been the best thing for her in the long run. A few minutes of embarrassment may have saved her from years of heartache.

Grooms are not the only people who get nervous at weddings. At another wedding the best man stole the show. The Unity candles were near him and the air conditioning system kept blowing out one of the candles. Even though the ceremony was in progress, he grabbed his lighter and began relighting the candle. Every time the candle went out, out popped his trusty lighter. Whether his friends got married or not, the best man had made up his mind that candle was going to stay lit!

And then there was the time some of the fellows put shrimp in the hubcaps of the lucky couple's car . . .

No don't feel sorry for us preachers. Along the way we have lots of fun, probably more than most folks. And the next time you attend a wedding, pay attention and you might get in on some of the fun that a lot of people miss.

One Clever Way To Prove You Are A Real Man

Someone asked me if I was serious about learning how to chew Red Man chewing tobacco. So I reckon I need to explain why I am thinking about it.

I know that chewing tobacco is risky business, and that it may be one cause of cancer. I understand also that the genteel crowd thinks it is a prety nasty habit, and it is.

Why, there is hardly a man anywhere who can spit that juice out of his mouth without having some of it dribble down on his chin. That really is no problem; a fellow who is reasonably alert can wipe it on his shirt sleeve before it does any damage.

But if a fellow is a little slow, like a lot of us are, it can ruin a shirt a day. Even so that problem can be overcome too. You can just get a few of these new, ugly ties and wear them. These new ties look like they were designed by two cats fighting in fresh paint, and a little tobacco juice would help most of them.

One reason I feel tempted to start chewing tobacco is that some of my best friends chew. I love to hear them talk about how good it is to get out in the woods, where there are no white carpets and no fussing folks, and cut down on a big chew.

Herman visited my friend, Robert, down at Perdue Hill recently. He said they found a spot on a hillside out in the country, with a gentle breeze blowing. There they sat on a log together, forgetting for awhile the cares of the world, just chewing, spitting, and dribbling. It made my mouth water just listening to Herman describe the good time they had.

As they tell us in that familiar beer commercial, "it just doesn't get any better than this," sitting on a log in Perdue Hill, chewing and spitting Red Man. What a life!

It reminds me of that fellow who insisted on being buried in his pink Cadillac. As the preacher said some words over him, there he was, sitting behind the wheel, in his best suit, still wearing his big diamond rings, dead as a hammer.

Family and friends stared in amazement as they lowered the man, car and all, into a deep grave. When the preacher was done, one man remarked to another, "Man, that's really living!"

His remark came spontaneously from that innate desire in all of us to really live. And all our lives we have been influenced by ingenious advertising schemes designed to persuade us that "real living" comes through buying and using certain products.

My brain, like all the rest, has been bombarded with not so subtle suggestions that "real men" use Brut, drive fancy cars, drink Bud, wear faded jeans, fight off drooling women, and chew Red Man.

Naturally preachers, a few of us being male, have a craving to be thought of as real men. We don't want our parishioners to think we are sissies who enjoy sitting around telling little old ladies in tennis shoes how much we love the flowers. So some of us do strange things trying to convince people that we truly are he-men — things like yelling lustily at football games, going deer hunting at four o'clock in the morning, running for exercise, and driving old-model green trucks.

We have learned from the presidential campaigns how important image-building is, so we work hard to project ourselves as virile, robust, red-blooded men. Now it is hard enough for a pastor to build a "real man" image, but it is even harder when a bishop makes him a district superintendent.

Then you really have your work cut out for you. The funny thing about it is that most pastors hunger after the honor of becoming a "DS," as we Methodists call them, and immediately after receiving the honor they begin to complain secretly to fellow pastors that nobody in his right mind would want such a job.

They want their fellow pastors to ache for them and to understand that serving as a "DS" is something equivalent to being sent to the African bush country as an underpaid missionary. "Show us some sympathy," they plead with their pastors, "and remember, the day may come when you will have to take your turn serving in this dreadful position. You can't imagine how tough a job this is until you have to sit around that table with the bishop and the other men who are making the sacrifice to serve in his cabinet."

One of my friends, who is now a "combat veteran" of cabinet service, learned quickly from a layman in his district how to convince folks that he was a real man. You guessed it; it was the Red Man technique.

"Before you go out to one of your country churches to hold your first church conference," this layman suggested, "buy two pouches of Red Man. Empty out a hunk from one of them and replace it with a wad of raisins."

"Then, in full view of everybody, just before you begin the meeting, pull out that pouch of Red Man, reach in and get those raisins, and put them in your mouth. Chew on them for a few minutes, and then, looking at everybody, swallow that wad of raisins with a gulp."

"When you have done that," he said, "wipe your mouth on your coat sleeve and call the meeting to order. Those folks will know they are dealing with a real man, and your reputation will quickly spread across the district. From that day forward, nobody will mess with you because they'll know that instead of a sissy preacher, they have a tough dude in the driver's seat."

The last time I saw my friend Bob was still carrying two pouches of Red Man in his pocket. Why the second pouch? Obviously so you can be ready to offer other real men a hunk of the real thing.

You can understand now why I am tempted to try the Red Man plan. My only hesitation is that I know I will have to be mighty careful to convince my wife that it really is raisins I'm chewing. At my age, having had to give up on a lot of things, I simply can't afford to give up kissing too.

After all, as much as I want the "real man" image, I am no fool. There is just no way that chewing tobacco could ever take the place of kissing.

As much as I hate to admit it, I guess I'll have to come up with a better plan for becoming a real man. I have never liked raisins that much anyway.

Why Preachers Sometimes Disappear

"When you really need a preacher, you can't find one!"

That's how one of my church members greeted me the other day. He was still frustrated several days later because when he had a problem, he couldn't locate me. And that's not an uncommon problem.

It happens sometimes when you need your doctor. His answering service says he's not available this weekend, but Dr. Freckle Bomb is taking his calls. And for all you know Freckle Bomb may be a veterinarian.

Now we all know that physicians work under so much intense pressure that they have to have some time off. We can understand that. But preachers live the life of Riley so yours ought to be available whenever you need him. I want to explain why you cannot always find your preacher.

First, we like to create the impression that we have to get away to some spiritual hideaway to talk to God. There, as God spoke to Moses on Mount Sinai, He gives us our sermons so that when we enter the pulpit each Sunday we have a word straight from the Lord.

But we are afraid that sort of explanation might sound too spiritual to the average person. So we come up with more ingenious answers. Pierce Harris, the preacher whose name was a household word for years in Atlanta, named the rooms of his home for several states. When he was studying, and did not want to receive phone calls, he had his wife say, "He is in Florida today." Actually he was in his study, which he had named "Florida."

Another preacher named his boat "Calls." When he was fishing, his secretary would tell those who telephoned, "He is out on Calls right now."

One pastor thought that such a great idea that he asked his family to help him come up with a clever name for his boat. Since he had four kids, one of his boys suggested they call the boat "Six Pack." The preacher wisely nixed that name; only a fool would want his secretary to tell the deacons that the good reverend was off having fun with a six pack.

The second reason why we preachers practice our disappearing act is that, like everyone else, we don't enjoy facing the music. We have a special radar that lets us know when trouble is brewing and some of our critics are coming by. Now I ask you, which would you rather do: listen to somebody bellyache about a pet peeve, or go off somewhere and talk to God?

It really is a shame that, after a few years in the ministry, most of us preachers are gunshy about criticism. Some of it we need to hear; the constructive kind can help us. But if you get shot at too much, it affects your hearing. Strangely though it is not all that hard to hear an encouraging word from a gentle soul.

Preachers find it hard to have fun because we are afraid that our members may get the idea that we are shortchanging God or the church. The work ethic is deeply imbedded in most of us so subconsciously we believe we must work hard for God and our congregation to remain happy.

We tend to be like the old priest who was asked by a much younger priest, "Father, lately I keep thinking that the Lord's return is imminent, that Jesus could be coming back any day now. What should I do?" The old priest replied simply, "Look busy!"

So we try to stay busy doing religious work, thus avoiding the unpleasant task of facing the music before a displeased God or our unhappy church brethren.

Now the next time you call your preacher and the secretary says he's in Florida or out on calls, don't blow a gasket. Take a few deep breaths, smile, and remember that your God is such a great God that he can even help you sometimes without having to pipe his grace through a preacher.

And don't spend a lot of time wondering if your preacher really is in Florida or not. He may be out climbing Mount Sinai looking for a fresh word of inspiration for next Sunday. He may be out fishing, or playing golf, or spending some time with his family.

If so you can give thanks that you have a smart preacher. For one thing is certain: too much church work, like too much cholesterol, can be damaging to your health.

Nothing about our son David's illness had caused us to suspect that bad news was forthcoming. The only warning we had was the unusual request from our doctor for both of us to meet him at 9 a.m. the next morning in a conference room at the hospital. But even that did not trigger great alarm in our minds.

We assumed that David's problem was merely one of the many childhood diseases that we knew about, like chicken pox or measles. We were bothered but not troubled deeply, even though several tests had turned up negative. The latest test had been a sternum puncture, requiring hospitalization, but we had not been advised why this test was being made.

Though no one else would have reason to remember that day, Dean and I remember well the 28th morning of September that year. Shown to the room by a gracious nurse, we sat silently waiting for the doctor.

Soon Dr. T. Forte Bridges came in, greeted us in his gentle manner, and got right to the point. "I regret that I have disturbing news for you," he said, without smiling. "The test results have confirmed my suspicion that your son has acute leukemia."

We sat there stunned in disbelief, speechless. I did not recall ever having heard the word "leukemia" before that moment. So I asked him to explain this illness to us. I don't remember what he said. I am sure he said it was a type of cancer which affects the blood.

What I do remember so well is that his concluding words were, "Unfortunately, there is no known cure for this type of leukemia." My heart sank. I felt unbelievably helpless. It felt like I had been hit between the eyes with a sledgehammer.

"You mean he is going to die?" I stammered. "Yes, I am afraid so," he replied, "unless a cure is found very soon. There is a lot of medical research going on, so there is always a chance that a remedy will be discovered."

"How much time does David have?" I asked, dreading his answer.

"There is no way to know for sure," Doctor Bridges said. "My best guess is that he has from two months to two years."

Sensing our utter helplessness, the kind doctor continued: "All we can do now is to make him as comfortable as possible, and pray that a cure may be found in time."

A few minutes later we broke the terrible news to our family. I can still remember how blurred the trees looked as I walked outside the hospital. Looking up into a cloudy sky, my heart breaking as I wondered why God had allowed this to happen to us.

After all, we loved God. I had just begun my second year in the divinity school at Vanderbilt, having committed my life to the ministry while a student at Auburn. At this point in my life "the suffering of the innocent" had been no more than a casual subject for study.

Now we were caught up in it personally. We had to deal with tough questions we had never faced. One was the usual, "Why me, God?" But we would face many deeper and more burning questions quickly.

We learned later that the suffering and death of a child often results in the divorce of the parents. While that did not happen to us, our marriage was severely strained by the experience. We reacted differently, both to the suffering and to David's death. We coped with grief differently, which was not unusual, but it meant that we were not as understanding and supportive of each other as we might have been.

I prayed that God would heal David. Dean prayed that God would give us the strength to handle our pain. God answered both our prayers. He said "No" to me, but blessed me as well by providing the help for which Dean prayed.

I thought at first that God's answer was an unfeeling, uncaring *no*. I felt often the surge of anger and bitterness within me.

When it became obvious that David was going to die, I was on the verge of turning harsh and bitter. There seemed no sense in it at all. If God was really love, as the Bible teaches, and if he was truly omnipotent, then why would he allow our precious little boy to die?

David was three years old, bright-eyed, intelligent, and full of energy, with blue eyes and blond hair. Life was just beginning for him. He had done no wrong, so why should he suffer such pain and death? Why? My brain burned with the question: Why?

Nine months after our morning with Doctor Bridges, David died in my arms at sunrise, after a long and sleepless night. We buried him on a crisp day in May about a month after his third birthday.

Now and then someone will ask, "How long did it take you to get over David's death?" I have learned to explain that you don't get "over" it, you just find strength to go on. Mainly you discover that God helps you to get through it.

The pain remains, but somehow the hurt is gradually healed. You learn to understand that God does not will such illness and suffering; instead he hurts with you and helps you learn how to hang on and become a better person.

Each of us is free to become bitter or better by the way we respond to life's misfortunes. I am thankful that somehow we managed not to indulge ourselves long in bitterness.

We still do not have answers to life's hard questions. But we have found that we can know God, and we are sure that knowing God is better than knowing answers.

We have faced even tougher problems since those days when David was dying. And somehow God helped us to find a way to tie a knot in our rope and hold on until help came.

Some folks call it coping. I like to think of it as faith, faith that grows, and faith that helps us keep on believing against all odds that behind everything there is a loving heavenly Father who is constantly working for our good.

When The Preacher Talks On And On

One Sunday at lunch my wife told me gently that she felt my sermon was a little long. After all these years, I know what she really meant, and it had nothing at all to do with a clock.

She meant the sermon was a bit dull, and that I should have worked on it more. Bless her heart, she was right. I knew that I had not prepared as fully as I should have, and the quality of the sermon was not up to par.

Actually, a boring sermon is too long even if it lasted only 10 minutes. A good sermon may last an hour and not be considered too long.

What my wife considers a good sermon is one which includes a couple of interesting, compelling stories. She knows that Jesus was a terrific preacher and he was a master at telling stories to make a point about the kingdom.

So I am always looking for good stories, since they can truly "make" a fine sermon. And it is so refreshing to have people relate to you later, using one of your stories as a point of reference.

Sunday, for example, I told about a preacher who apologized in the pulpit for the band-aid on his face. He said, "I was thinking about my sermon while shaving and cut my face." Later he found a note left in the offering plate, "Next time, think about your face and cut your sermon."

I was making the point that some folks do not need much preaching. They are satisfied with themselves. One sermon a month is enough for some folks. And we even have a few people who need no more than one or two sermons a year.

On the other hand, there are those who are seeking — more grace, more spiritual food, more understanding of God's Word. These dear ones are folks who feel, "The more we receive from the Lord, the more we want." They have a hunger for more of God.

You can imagine how thrilled I was, then, when a man walked up to me Sunday night and said, "Preacher, as far as I am concerned you can cut your face all you want, just don't cut your sermons! They really mean a lot to me."

The glow of a word of encouragement like that can linger for six months in my memory, and bless my waking moments every time I think about it.

Paul must have had some long sermons. When he was preaching in Troas one night, Luke tells us that a young man named Eutychus sank into "a deep sleep as Paul talked on and on (Acts 20:9)." And, Luke says, "When he was sound asleep, he fell to the ground from the third story."

Maybe that is why most Methodists build their churches on the ground level, so the modern cousins of Eutychus will not have so far to fall.

If your preacher has a tendency to "talk on and on," give him a few good stories, maybe about the time you got caught selling moonshine, or stealing watermelons. Then if he works up a good sermon around one of your stories, tell him how glad you are that he kept you awake.

Who knows, you may get to liking your pastor's preaching so much that you'll tell him what Leroy told me, not to cut my sermons even if I cut my face. Just be near a hospital when you tell him; he may have a heart attack.

Free To Sit On A Pumpkin

The waters of Walden Pond stirred some right interesting thoughts in the mind of Henry David Thoreau. One which catches my attention as we observe the Fourth of July is this:

"I would rather sit on a pumpkin, and have it all to myself, than to be crowded on a velvet cushion."

I am not sure I agree with Brother Henry, though we can give thanks that in America we are free to sit on pumpkins. That is assuming, of course, that it is our pumpkin we are sitting on.

In this great land of the free, one may head to the privacy of the woods and exchange the honking of horns for the sweet merriment of the birds. I have always thought I would have enjoyed being with Thoreau, but that would have spoiled his adventure in solitude. He would not have wanted me along. I know, for he once said, "I never found the companion that was so companionable as solitude."

I imagine it would have been fun to talk with him. I love to talk with people who really think, who are willing to get beneath the surface, past the superficial, childish level of living. It is not important that everyone agrees with me. In fact, I find a difference of opinion exciting; it challenges my own understanding, and makes me think a bit deeper, always seeking the solid rock of truth, for no one has a corner on the truth. Total grasp of reality is available to no one.

Thoreau understood the importance of doing what you really love to do, instead of whiling away the years doing some monotonous thing you hate doing. It is inspiring to meet a person who has given up one profession for another simply because the former work was not fulfilling and satisfying. Only a fool is willing to work at something for his whole life that he really does not want to do at all. That is a misuse of the gift of life since most of us are relatively free to choose work that brings us some degree of satisfaction.

Determined to "suck the marrow" from the bones of life, Thoreau insisted, "Do what you love. Know your own bone; gnaw at it, bury it, unearth it, and gnaw it still." Do not merely exist, he said. Find out what living really is for you, and then go for it. Find your bone and gnaw on it! What a vivid way to express a terrific idea! Life indeed is sweetest "near the bone."

Thoreau's cynicism might have been hard to stomach. He once observed that he had received no more than one or two letters in his whole life that were "worth the postage." Imagine what he would say if he had to fight his way through all the junk mail of our day!

Some of his insights strike fire with my spirit. Sick of the hollowness of life, he discovered some important principles for living. "Money," he said, "is not required to buy one necessity of the soul." Some folks think money can buy anything, that every person has "a price." But surely it is true that the best things in life do not have a price tag. "That man," Thoreau said, "is the richest whose pleasures are the cheapest."

Reading, for example, is one of those marvelous things which one may do without spending a lot of money. We can expose our minds to not only the splendid ideas of the Bible, but to many other books which will make us rich in understanding. That in turn can lead us into joyous and fulfilling adventures in the art of living.

Since we are flooded with so many books today, we might do well to heed Thoreau's advice: "Read the best books first, or you may not have a chance to read them at all."

So give thanks as we celebrate the privileges of living in the land of the free and the home of the brave. If you wish, you may sit on a pumpkin.

Thoreau preferred sitting on a pumpkin alone to sitting with a crowd on a velvet cushion. He did not like crowds; solitude was the name of his game. We can all understand his feeling; there are times when we all feel that way.

As for me, I would rather take the pumpkin home and let Mamma make some pumpkin pies, then enjoy the fellowship of my family and friends. A crowd is not so bad, even on a velvet cushion, if you are with people you love.

Who knows, Thoreau might have even learned something from me if he had taken the time out of his "dismal swamp" to listen. Real living is not so much a bone to gnaw on, as a journey home, a time for sharing joy and sorrow with friends and loved ones, a time for crying and singing, a time for caring and cooking, a time for learning from one another how the Father wants us to live.

I would bet my last dollar that Thoreau did want a crowd in one way, a crowd of folks to buy his books on solitude. How else could he buy a pumpkin?

Freedom is a precious commodity. Choose wisely how you will spend it. The Great Pumpkin is watching.

Just Bury Me In My Old Pickup Truck

My life has really changed since I bought my old pickup truck. As I ride around town in it I know I must be the envy of every man in Lee County.

It's a Ford pickup, which suits me fine since I am a Fuller Ford man. I knew it was mine when I saw a tattered old Fuller Ford sticker on the rear bumper.

My truck is one of the "Explorer" series, and I like that too. That sounds like the name of a space ship, and it stirs thoughts of adventure and excitement. I enjoy exploring, whether woods or ideas. Considering some of the dumb names the auto makers have given their vehicles in recent years, "Explorer" has to rank as one of the best.

The driver's manual says my truck has a 302 engine. That means nothing to me, except that some fellows say that is one of the best engines ever made. So I tell people it has a 302 engine just like I know what I'm talking about. I figure most folks are like me; they hate to admit that they don't know what a 302 engine is either. All other things being equal, I guess it must be a little better than a 301 engine, one better anyway.

My truck has "five-way" air conditioning. I can have hot air in the summer and cold air in the winter. All I have to do is open the vent under the dashboard, roll down the windows, and push open the two small windows. Then I have all the air I need. And being a preacher, I am never without hot air anyway.

By now you may have guessed that my truck is one of the newer models. It is a smart 1972 model. The body is in very good shape. The engine is clean, and there is not much rust on the bed. In fact, the bed does not have even a small hole in it.

Before I bought the truck, I always had something I needed to haul somewhere. Now that I have it, I don't seem to have anything to haul. The only thing I have hauled lately has been rainwater. Since the bed has no holes in it, I have a good load of water after each rain, which I distribute up Eighth Street on my way to the church.

My Explorer has the old fashioned "ALLYOUGOT" power steering. It takes all the strength I've got to turn the wheel, especially on close corners. That is good, though, because it means I don't have to belong to a health club. I get plenty of exercise just driving my truck. During the summer I can leave the windows up and it's like a sauna. That truck makes my body dream up new ways to sweat.

I would hang my rifle in it like real men do, except I don't have a rifle. We spent my rifle money raising our four sons. I have been tempted to put a coffee can on the floor and learn to spit Red Man juice in it, but Dean says that would mean the end of kissing, and I don't believe I could ever like chewing tobacco as much as I do kissing.

Since I don't care a whole lot for dogs, I have been wondering about getting one of those marble Dalmation dogs to sit in the back. But those things probably cost too much, and if I got one, every other red-blooded pickup owner in Lee County would want one. You have to be careful about starting a new fad.

On the cab I have three yellow lights which seem to be burned out. Then I have a nice air horn which is not hooked up to the battery. I have an idea the previous owner's wife told him she was going to leave him if he didn't stop blowing that horn all the time. My wife has told me she may kill me if I ever get the horn to work and start blowing it all over town.

What I really want to do is to see if I can find a way to make the horn blow the Auburn fight song, so I can let my Bama friends hear that when I pass them. Then I want to see if I can get it to play "Amazing Grace." What a truck that would be!

In case you have not seen it, the color of my truck is a lovely light green. Actually, it is a putrid green to my wife, but beauty is, after all, in the eye of the beholder. She keeps pushing me to get it painted light blue.

The chances of that happening are slim to none. I would not trust a man who let his wife tell him what color to paint his truck. On this I have decided to stand my ground. She has been pushing colors on me all my life. She decides what color to paint the bedroom, the den, even the outside of the house. But I have my limits, and I simply am not going to ride around this town in a truck painted baby blue. She can tell me what color ties to wear, but my truck is going to stay green.

I am thinking about leaving instructions for the undertaker to bury me in my pickup truck. In Nashville I had a sportswriter friend who wrote a book about his life and titled it, *Bury Me In An Old Press Box.*'' He had spent a lot of his life in press boxes and it seemed to be a clever idea.

It's not a new idea really. I heard about a farmer in Georgia who told his preacher he wanted to be buried in his old pickup truck. When the preacher asked why, he said, ''Because I never got in a hole yet that this old truck couldn't get me out of!''

But, if Dean decides against burying me in my pickup, I will understand. After all, with this pickup in her front yard, she will be the most sought after woman in the county. With a little luck some old codger will come along who will enjoy taking her and my truck to antique shows all over the country.

I waited 59 years to have my own pickup truck, and I have wanted one all my life. I learned how to drive when I was eight years old — in my father's pickup truck on our farm. Dad let me drive while he threw off hay to feed the cows. I was proud of that, but I got too cocky and broke a calf's leg one day trying to show my cousin how well I could drive.

Now that I have it, I'm going to enjoy my truck. After all, what is life without a little fun? In a few years I may use my truck to earn a few extra bucks for my retirement. I believe fellows who don't have one might pay me five or 10 dollars a night to have me park my truck in their front yard.

If you think I've gone overboard about my truck, just remember it could be worse. Some folks are crazy about pet rocks.

Simple Folks Are My Kind Of Folks

I like common folks, people who speak plainly, who don't try to put on a show for you. For my money, these are the real people of the world, honest folk who have lost the need to pretend.

Some folks are so given to sham that you can hardly distinguish the real person from the pretense. These people make an art of appearing to be *somebody* — when they are not!

These pretenders act like they are smarter than they are, or that they have money they really don't have. They like to drop names on you, wanting you to believe that they've played the horses with Pete Rose or somebody.

Now I'm not saying that simple folks are less intelligent than other people. To be simple, is not to be simpleminded. Simple folks are just plain folks, free of any affectation.

I don't mind listening to a fellow talk if he really knows what he is talking about. One of my friends talk about neutrons and protons as easily as a farmer might speak about making sorghum syrup. That's fine.

But what makes me want to get off the bus is to have somebody chime in, wanting the rest of us to believe that he is an expert on splitting the atom when the truth is, he barely knows how to split a log to go on the fire.

Simple folks can wear an old shirt down to the restaurant to drink coffee with you. They don't have to "dress up" so as to impress you.

Bankers and preachers are afflicted with the same curse. Their wives all want them to "look the part," so most of us go around town wearing these stupid neckties and business suits.

Wearing ties is just about the dumbest thing that men have ever learned to do. What you have is a strange piece of cloth knotted around your neck in such a way that it causes a hard collar to rub your skin raw.

I would say the tie is useless except that it does help to catch gravy, so you don't stain your shirt. But then it stains your tie, and you have to pay an arm and a leg to get it cleaned.

Somebody should come out with a disposable bib for men, then maybe we could persuade our wives to let us stop wearing these blooming ties.

My friend Bob does use a bib of sorts. He gracefully spreads his napkin over his tie when he eats out. He is not the least embarrassed about it.

"This silk tie cost me $40," he told me, "so I am not about to let food drop on it."

I told him it's bad enough to have to wear a tie in the first place, but it's even worse to wear one that is so expensive you cannot enjoy a meal without worrying about it.

That is one problem I don't plan to have. I'm not going to pay $40 for a tie as long as Wal-Mart stays in business. And if someone gives me an expensive silk tie, I'll swap it for the money and use the money to go bowling. Thank God, you don't see many ties at the bowling alley.

It is commonly said that one of our preachers is so addicted to a necktie, that his wife has never seen him come to breakfast in his own home without one. Lord, that sounds stuffy! I have often wondered if he *sleeps* with a tie on.

Call that same preacher on the telephone, and you have a surprise in store. When his wife answers the phone, and you ask if Tom is in, she will reply "Just one moment, please, and I'll see if Doctor Pomposity can speak to you."

Now his name really is Tom, but his wife cannot allow the dear man to be just old Tom. She has to remind you that some college crowned him with an honorary doctor's degree, and that he is thus a notch above the common crowd. If you are anything like me, by now you don't give a hoot about talking to brother Tom.

I enjoy using stories that people can understand to convey the eternal truths of the Gospel. Preaching that folks cannot understand may be impressive, but it's about as useful as a saddle on a billy goat.

One woman told me she liked my preaching because it was so down to earth. I told her that at one time, as a young preacher, I had tried to preach lofty, sophisticated sermons, but I failed. So I decided to stick with "earthy" preaching, since it was as high as I could get, and that most people live down on the earth anyway.

I like to think that if Jesus were among us today, He would tell stories about bird dogs and caterpillars. I think people would understand Him just like the Pharisees did long ago, when He looked them squarely in the eye and called them a bunch of hypocrites.

They knew He was sick of their pretense and sham. And they knew that God would be pleased if they would stop pretending and just live like real people.

One thing is for sure, God must love simple folks because He made a lot of them. I guess that's why simple folks are my kind of folks.

Conversations At The Altar

A little fellow about five smiled at me the other day. He was at the altar rail of our church, kneeling between his parents to receive Holy Communion. I winked at him, and he gave me an even broader smile.

I love to watch the little people as they kneel at the altar. They are not sure why they are there. They are just following the example of their parents, and wondering what it all means. Sometimes they pray with their eyes open, but surely God does not frown at that.

I am so glad that little boy is learning to kneel at the altar. His parents are teaching him many things, but none may be more important than to develop the habit of kneeling before God.

Eventually that boy, who is not bothered at all by tough questions just now, will discover that at the altar he can find answers to all of life's perplexing questions. He can receive there God's help as he wrestles with the questions of why he is alive, whom he is to marry, and what he is to do with his life.

Over the years I have had many conversations at the altar with people who were doing business with God. These have been some of the most memorable moments of my life. A pastor has the honor of simply "being there" when many boys and girls, men and women, decide to resign as general manager of the universe and let God take over the guidance of their lives.

I realize that one can do business with God at any place one chooses — on a stump in the woods, on a golf course, or while watching a beautiful sunset. But the altar of a church, erected to the glory of God, seems like one of the best places for a good talk with the Lord.

I have seen many people make decisions at the altar which resulted in changed lives, relationships knit back together, and new directions for living clarified.

Many churches like my own have a kneeling rail, which appeals to me. I know it is the attitude of the heart which really matters, but it seems so appropriate to kneel before God as an expression of humility. It symbolizes our inward submission to the One who has given us life and all good things.

Since pride is such a problem for everyone, to kneel at the altar is a way of saying, "Father, I humble myself before you, and invite you to speak to me what I need most to hear. I am willing to listen to you, and to obey you, in all things." When a person comes before God in that spirit, life is soon shifted into overdrive!

One Sunday morning a quiet-spoken man got up out of his seat in our choir and knelt at the altar rail during the hymn of invitation. As his pastor I knew him well. He was shy, but a faithful member of our church.

Later he explained why he went forward. "I had not planned to go," he said, "but while we were singing the closing hymn, I felt God speaking to me. He was saying, 'It is time for you to step forward and make a public commitment of your life to me. You have stood quietly in the shadows long enough.' "

He had been troubled for some time about his timidity. He knew there were times when "letting his light shine" was not enough — that he needed to become free to share verbally his love for Christ. Going to the altar was a step forward in faith, a symbol of his new willingness to learn to verbalize his faith.

I watched that man closely during the months that followed. He did not change overnight. But gradually he emerged from his shell. He learned to share what was happening inside himself with a prayer group and with a Sunday school class. He had a new spirit, a new joy, as he discovered God could use his words as well as his example to attract others to the Kingdom. His full potential was being released slowly by the Spirit of God.

Explain it any way you want, but the man's new life sprang from a talk with God at the altar.

Dan and Sylvia found a way to forge a life together within their family after a trip to the altar one night. Dan's quiet stubbornness was dissolved as he and Sylvia began to pray together with their children.

Charles and Winnie, who were married one night while they were drunk, knelt with me at the altar one morning. They had endured 25 stormy years of marriage but now wanted to put the past behind them, and ask God to bless their union.

I asked them to take their wedding rings off and give them to me. Then I led them through the marriage ritual, exchanging vows and rings, and placing the rings on each other's finger again, this time in the name of Christ. Years later they told me that trip to the altar saved their marriage.

The altar can be a wonderful place of beginning again.

Recalling The Summer Of '54

Few of us will forget this first summer of the '90s. It has been so hot and dry I have almost forgotten what rain looks like. But I still remember the drought of the summer of 1954, and how miserable the weather was then.

Dean and I were completing our first year in the ministry and I was finishing my education at Auburn. We were living in a simple home in Macon County, near Bradford's Chapel, one of four Methodist churches I was pastoring.

Like most folks out there we got our water from a private well beside the house. But rain was so scarce that the well dried up and we had to haul water in for a few weeks. As the water level dropped, we found it tasted worse and worse. So I had it tested.

The report came back in the mail, informing us that the water contained "fecal matter." It was the first time I had ever seen that phrase; we used other words for feces over in Elmore County where I grew up.

That report caused the trustees to realize that the well and the septic tank were too close together. Happily, by summer's end, we had a new well with plenty of uncontaminated water.

Early that summer I had planted a garden, using a borrowed mule from a good Baptist neighbor. I wanted to prove to my church members that I really was a country boy. It didn't prove anything though, except that without rain my garden, like most others, was burned to a crisp by mid-July. Anyway one old man said the way I talked was evidence enough that I had not been off the farm too long.

Even though I had grown up on a farm, the folks in that rural community made me realize I had a lot to learn. One thing was about how farm folks take care of their preacher. They did not pay a big salary; we received $1,900 that year. But the way people looked after us helped us discover that the preacher's best pay is not dollars anyway.

Those folks loved us far beyond our deserving. It wasn't sloppy or demeaning love either. Old Hoyt liked to call and say, "You got any snuff?" He really didn't use it, it was just his way of finding out if we were home. In a few minutes he would come over with a mess of peas, corn, or sweet potatoes.

He never said he knew we were hungry, but I can't help but wonder now if some of those times he may have known that what he brought us was all the food we had. You never really know how good squash can taste until the day your cupboard is bare, and suddenly two loving hands are at the door with a dish of squash, already cooked!

Farm folks may call on you rather early though. One morning about 5 a.m. we were awakened by a pounding on the door so loud that I knew someone had died. But standing at the door, grinning because he knew he had gotten me out of bed, was one of the Segrest brothers. Shoving a big sack of turnip greens toward me, he said, "Preacher, you do know how to wash 'em, don't you?"

Every community is bound to have a jerk or two in it, and Milstead was no exception. One sweet woman in one church had a sour old husband who was mad with God and everybody, and he despised preachers. He got his kicks out of trying to make you feel like a fool, and he knew naturally that all preachers were fools.

One day when we visited him and his family, he ignored us for the most part, trying to appear busy with his chores. Then as we started to leave, he handed me a paper sack with a cured ham inside. He was doing what appeared to be a loving deed, but his face was screwed up like he had just swallowed a green persimmon.

His words are hard to forget: "Preacher, this here ham is for your poor wife and baby; you could get you a job and earn some money and buy you something to eat." Repartee comes easy for me, but that day I was stunned, humiliated, and speechless. I drove away seething, thinking of things I wish I had been quick enough to say. I know now that he was a miserable man who in some way was reaching out to me for help. I wish I had been wise enough to have helped him.

We left Milstead after Christmas that year, and my memories of those dear people grow fonder with each passing year. They made 1954 a great year in our lives.

But that hot, dry summer I don't enjoy remembering. So, please, Lord, let it rain again in Opelika, soon.

Being A Sermon Is Harder Than Preaching One

E. Stanley Jones was 77 when I first met him. The occasion was a retreat in Silver Springs, Florida, in which Jones was the featured speaker.

I was captivated by his wit, brilliance, and amazing energy. Highly disciplined, Jones arose each morning at 5:30 no matter what time he had gone to bed. Whenever possible he was in bed by 10 p.m.

He spoke of God in ways that appealed to me greatly. For Jones God was not just some distant "Creator." He was a caring Father, present with us, and ready to give us companionship daily. He even reacts to us in practical, sensible ways.

One example of God's good sense came out of the story Jones told of being up one night until 3 a.m. because of air travel delays. Though exhausted he struggled out of bed to keep his appointment with God at 5:30 a.m. He called this time his "listening post."

As soon as he began to listen to the Lord, Jones said, the Lord spoke to him quite clearly. "Stanley," the Lord said, "go back to bed; you need some more sleep."

I believe in a God like that, and it helped me so much to learn from this unusual author and missionary that it was all right to think of God as having ordinary common sense. For too many people God is a theological equation or an oblong blur. It helps most of us to understand that God has as much good judgment as a wise, old grandfather, and a whole lot more.

That week with Jones in Florida was a turning point in my life. I learned to trust God more, and received as a gift of grace the calm assurance of my own salvation. My wife and I both entered into a deeper walk with Christ, a walk that began to affect our marriage and our ministry in marvelous ways.

Since then Jones has been a mentor and model for me. Through tapes and books, he has been a constant source of inspiration for me.

Jones was a health nut and always carried a bag of apples with him, his substitute for junk food. He cheerfully recommended grace, grass (vitamins), and gumption as the secret of a healthy mind and body.

"Brother Stanley," as he insisted we call him, enjoyed good health into his 87th year. For over 50 years he preached around the world this basic message: life is at its best only when "Jesus is Lord!"

He insisted on a "benedictine silence" at night during his retreats. The silence would be broken each morning as we came to Bible study before breakfast with his motto, the earliest of all Christian creeds, "Jesus is Lord!"

Before reaching his 88th birthday, Jones suffered a paralyzing stroke. Without warning his sight, hearing, speech, and locomotion were suddenly impaired. His family and friends may have wondered, now that tragedy had befallen him, could he continue to affirm that Jesus is the divine Yes of God?

Jones could, and he would. With unbelievable willpower, he began to write his final book. Its title you may have guessed: "The Divine Yes!"

His doctors said he would never walk again. But he did. His doctors said he would never preach again. But he did.

Against impossible odds, Jones recovered sufficient strength to preach again, and more than that, to become a demonstration of his preaching through his courageous spirit.

"Perhaps," he said, "I can write this book by faith. If it is now hard for me to preach a sermon, why not *be* one?" And he was! This man, who had once preached some of the most powerful sermons I have ever heard, became himself a marvelous sermon to behold.

All of us would rather "see a sermon than hear one." Maybe that's because it is a whole lot harder to be a good sermon than to preach one.

If you see a good one now and then, give thanks. In a lifetime, most of us will hear a lot more sermons than we will see. But then, it may not take but one or two good ones to turn your heart toward home.

Sleeping In Church

If I live to be 100 I will never forget a little mutt we had when our children were growing up. We lived in Pensacola where I was serving in my first pastorate out of seminary. After four years in Auburn, two at Vanderbilt, and one at Emory, I thought my education was completed. I soon discovered it was only beginning.

The completion of my academic work, plus two years of serving as a pastor in Midway, Alabama, had qualified me for that awesome experience of kneeling at an altar in Montgomery before a distinguished bishop of our church, Clare Purcell. Now barely 26 I had been licensed to preach for five years, but still knew little about how to do it.

Nevertheless the bishop ordained me, with the laying on of hands, and charging me with those historic words, "Take thou authority to preach the Word and administer the sacraments." With my appointment to Pine Forest Church in Pensacola, I was now fully authorized to go to my new congregation as "the pastor in charge."

It would have helped if someone had told me that if I was to have any authority, I would have to *take* it, for folks don't give it to you just because you have a title and degree. To use a phrase popular nowadays, "You have to earn it!" And so far as being "in charge," you quickly learn that you are only in control of whatever the people are willing for you to control — things like turning out the lights and locking up after everyone has gone home on Sundays, or making sure the heat or air is on when we all arrive at church.

But back to the mutt. We called him Snoozy because he enjoyed sleeping before the fire in the den so much. One hot August evening, while I was preaching the Word to our usual packed house with standing room only (forgive me, Lord!), Snoozy walked into the church. We lived just across the street, and since the doors were open because of the heat, it was a simple thing for Snoozy to come on over and check out my voice.

Standing in the pulpit, I was facing the door Snoozy came in and saw her immediately, though no one else did. They were all enraptured by my powerful sermon. (Well, you're right, they were just looking in my direction.) I continued preaching, watching Snoozy out of one eye. Slowly she kept coming, walking down the middle aisle. Realizing that the people would soon be distracted by her presence, on impulse I stopped preaching and spoke sharply to her, "Snoozy, go home!"

Immediately half the congregation was doubled up laughing out loud. When the laughing continued in spite of the serious "Let's get back to business" look on my face, I realized it was time for the benediction. Snoozy had obeyed me by leaving, but by now the people were in no mood for a sermon.

A few minutes later Tom English walked up grinning. His friend Amos Brewton, sitting next to him, had dozed off to sleep during my sermon. When I yelled out "Snoozy, go home," Tom thought I was talking about Amos. So he shook him awake, and said, "Wake up, the preacher's talking to you." Unbelieving, Amos replied out loud, "You're kidding!"

Nowadays whenever I see someone dozing in church during one of my dynamic sermons, I long to see Snoozy back in church again. The moral of this incident is simple: Be careful about sleeping in church; you may wake up the people sitting around you.

The Wisdom Of Listening To The Preacher

Preachers have to be careful what they say. In almost any church a few people are always listening. And the folks who pay attention are the ones who get you into trouble.

I love a good story and I've built whole sermons around one story that illustrates an important lesson in living. And a few times I have stretched a story or two to get a little more mileage out of them. I realized I was doing this one day when one of my teenage sons asked me, "Dad, that story you told in your sermon this morning: were you telling the truth or just preaching?" The family laughed so hard that I escaped without having to answer him, and just laughed with them.

Most preachers soon learn that not too many people are really listening to their sermons. Some are already on the golf course mentally, while others are reviewing plans for the coming week. The kids are drawing pictures (sometimes of the preacher), and the young people are passing notes. Some of my Methodist friends are hard to figure though; they have worked at it so long that they can appear to be awake when they are really half asleep. That's such a neat trick that you can't help but admire the ones who can do it.

Every preacher knows that the first sentence of a sermon is crucial. You want to grab the attention of your folks so they will be eager to hear the rest. Your introduction will either hook the audience or cause them to drop silently into passive boredom. But you must be careful not to overdo the beginning; too much use of the dramatic can result in overkill.

I learned this the hard way. One Sunday I began my sermon with these words: "Stand with me this morning with Moses on the muddy banks of the Red Sea." I had intended to go on and describe that dramatic moment Moses faced on that spot. The fearful Hebrew people were complaining about being taken out of Egypt into the wilderness, and in the distance

Moses saw the great cloud of dust indicating the advancing of Pharaoh's army of chariots. I wanted to praise the faith Moses demonstrated when he dared to trust God to part the waters of the sea so his people could walk across on dry ground and escape to freedom.

But by the time I had spoken the words, "Stand with me this morning . . .," to my surprise eight to 10 people suddenly stood up in the congregation! I was embarrassed, and they were too, and half the rest of the people had one hand on the pew in front of them, wondering if they should be standing also. Redfaced, I stopped and gently asked those standing to please be seated. Awkwardly I tried to thank those dear souls whose unexpected obedience had blown my introduction. Rather sheepishly I tried to recover some of my enthusiasm for my message.

Needless to say I have never begun another sermon with the words, "Stand with me." I learned a great lesson that Sunday. We preachers have to be very careful in our choice of words, especially those of us who have a flair for the dramatic. It may be hard to believe, but somebody may be listening and ready to respond!

Be Careful About Saying "Amen" In Church

Some people like to encourage the preacher with an occasional "Amen!" during his sermon. I don't object to it when I'm preaching. It is a clear sign that someone is in agreement with you and likes what you're saying. In fact I've noticed that if several folks start responding, it really pumps me up and helps me put my preaching in overdrive.

Some of my friends don't stop with amens; they like to say, "Hallelujah," or "Praise the Lord." But my personal, all-time favorite is a lusty "Glory!" Whenever I feel really overwhelmed by a blessing from God, I can hardly restrain from shouting "Glory!"

There are other folks who enjoy using phrases like "Tell it brother," "Well," "Yes," or "All right." I can't imagine what it would be like to have that kind of response on Sunday morning. Why I might get so fired up I wouldn't stop preaching until mid-afternoon. Not that I think I would have an audience that long, even though Methodists will let the preacher preach as long as he wants. They just go home about 12 o'clock.

Years ago I had a choir member who always sprinkled my sermons with strong amens. I found that unconsciously I was often pausing after major points, waiting for Jack's "amen." That worked fine for months and the congregation was accustomed to our rhythm.

But one Sunday it finally happened — I proclaimed the fourth point of my sermon and Jack remained silent when I paused! He couldn't "amen" my position. It was such an awkward moment that I even glanced at him along with most of the congregation. He was redfaced but defiant.

I have thought about Jack a lot over the years. Blunt and strongly opinionated, he was hard to get along with unless you agreed with his ideas. But he loved the Lord and you always knew where he stood. And even when we disagreed with each other, I felt he loved and respected me.

Now some Sundays when some of my folks are so quiet and still that they look like they were painted on the pews, I wish I still had Jack with me. He might liven things up a bit. But really what most of us preachers are looking for is not a loud "amen" but some indication that our preaching is making a difference and helping people to know God better. We want to know that our folks are "with" us, that they're really listening and that what we are saying is on the target of God's truth. We want to feel that our preaching is not warmed over pablum but gospel truth so relevant to daily living that it is sizzling hot and stirring people to respond to God.

I would a thousand times over rather have someone respond to God in a significant way than to shout a loud amen, or to say to me sweetly, "Nice talk, pastor." But the occasional amen is a good indicator that you are reaching one person, and if one, perhaps many more.

So next Sunday after your pastor gets into his sermon and makes a good point, haul off and shout "Amen, brother!" He will probably faint, and the ushers may want to escort you out. But when the preacher recovers he will likely preach the rest of his message with more vim and vigor. Just hope he is not preaching without notes as I do, or he may not remember his next point. Glory!

Wacky Ideas About Preachers

Preachers are strange ducks to some people. You have to laugh to keep from crying about some of the wacky ideas some folks have about us clerics.

"You only work one day a week." If I have heard that once, I have heard it a thousand times. How wrong can you get?

Anyone with a grain of sense should know that the average pastor works at least two days a week. In addition to Sunday's duties, he spends half a day consoling the people who are upset about something wrong that someone else did, and the rest of the day listening to the excuses of those who don't have time to do anything.

That doesn't include any time for writing sermons, which can take up to half an hour sometime. But who expects preachers to write sermons anyway? The bishop writes those for us, doesn't he, and if we haven't received a new one from headquarters by Saturday, we just preach an old one by Clovis Chappell or Charles Allen.

Then there are the dear ones who say, "I know you have never had a problem like this." Listen, we preachers have had every problem known to man, and a few more. Even those of us who are "deeply spiritual" are still human. We make fools of ourselves like everyone else. We hurt and cry just like all God's children do. But some of us put on a spiritual front because we think mistakenly that we are being paid to "be" spiritual.

We get tired of pretending that we are "on top of everything" all the time. But we are afraid no one would come to hear us preach if we admitted that we are just plain sick and tired — of anything. After all, we are supposed to *be happy* all the time since we are in the be happy business.

A few years ago I dared to share my broken heart with my congregation. Afterward a lady frowned at me and with great displeasure said, "It is so depressing to think that my pastor gets depressed."

I am sure she did not comprehend the irony of her comment. It was all right for her to be depressed; she was a real human being. But it was not acceptable for the preacher to be a real person since he is "the happy, holy one of God."

Come on, folks, give me a break. We preachers spill syrup on our pants, and catsup on our shirts, and now and then we even become angry and say things we don't mean. We can even become thickheaded when we are standing in that sacred place behind the pulpit. One Sunday a lady waved a dollar bill at me for 15 minutes and I thought she had lost her mind. After church she told me she was just trying to help me remember that I had forgotten to take up the offering! (No, that lady was not my wife, although she does hate for me to forget to receive the offering.)

Another wacky idea comes across from the folks who call you at nine o'clock in the morning and ask, "Are you up?" I have a suggestion here. Since most pastors have to get up by 10 every morning anyway, to do the milking and slop the hogs, why not wait until noon to phone so you can get right to the point of your call.

Perhaps the wackiest idea of all is that all preachers love to eat chicken. How absurd! That must be an old wives' tale. The truth is preachers just love to eat. But why pick on the poor chicken? I love turnip greens almost as well.

Some folks love to walk up to me and glancing at my middle, say, "Preacher, I can tell that's the graveyard for many a chicken!" I always smile because it's true. But it's true because most of the Methodists can't afford to buy their pastor a steak. Now the Baptists and the Episcopalians — I understand they eat a lot of steak and gravy.

Well, even if a few folks do have wacky ideas about us preachers, I wouldn't trade jobs with anybody. I love preaching and I am certain that the ministry is the place for me.

If you must know why I am so sure about my calling, I'll tell you. One morning when I was a young man I woke up with a terrible craving for fried chicken, and I didn't want to go to work.

Lots Of Crazy People

There are a lot of crazy people in this world. If you don't believe me, just ask any preacher. We meet them all. Every church has its share of neurotics around, though none of them would admit having a problem. They just seem to enjoy being a problem.

No wonder someone got so fed up with crazy folks that he said the earth must be the insane asylum of the universe.

When I lived in west Alabama I was asked to marry all kinds of folks, from high and low places. The wealthy usually make a wedding a show, using 179 candles, and turning the sanctuary into a garden center. You can almost forget that it is supposed to be a service of worship.

One family did not want to bother using the church; they insisted on a wedding in the back yard of their palatious home. At the rehearsal on Friday night half the bridal party was so drunk I could hardly finish the trial run.

With the scowl of John the Baptist on my face, I informed the bride and groom that I would not officiate at the wedding unless they promised there would be no more liquor until after the wedding. They agreed and I drove home feeling that once again righteousness had prevailed.

But was I in for a surprise! Everything went smoothly with the ceremony. I hardly noticed a refreshment bar well hidden behind some nearby bushes. As soon as I pronounced the beaming couple husband and wife, the groomsmen broke out the drinks — wine, beer, whiskey — enough to quench the thirst of an army. And food galore. The bride's parents must have shelled out a thousand bucks for the food and drinks alone.

The logical thing for me to have done was to leave. I am sure that was what the bridal party expected. But who wants to be logical all the time? I got a plate of food and stayed for

for an hour and a half. The longer I stayed the more I enjoyed it, watching some of my parishioners getting happy and trying to hide their drinks as they spoke to me.

One man saw me coming and quickly stuck his cocktail glass in his side coat pocket. As we shook hands I noticed it had spilled and was dripping down on his suit pants. He was a little embarrassed but too giddy to do more than blush and giggle.

But the craziest wedding I ever had took place at the rehearsal! As we gathered on Friday night to rehearse, the bride and groom and their friends were dressed in ugly, wild T-shirts. Before we began the groom walked up to me and asked if I would go ahead and marry them that night.

Seminary doesn't prepare you to know how to answer such a request. But sometimes you just have to trust God and go with the flow, so I said, "Sure, if it suits you, it's fine with me." Twenty minutes later they were married and on their way — a day early for their honeymoon.

The parents were perplexed but that was not the first time those two children had given them a headache. I imagine they were greatly relieved to have them "out of the nest" and on their own.

Before we condemn too quickly the crazy folks of this world, we must remember that some of them are paid megabucks to act crazy on television. Perhaps those who march to a different drum beat are not so crazy after all. They are just preparing for a great career in Hollywood or, dare I say it, in politics!

Some Of God's Dumbest Creatures

Preachers are some of God's dumbest creatures. Now I know some folks will argue with me about this. They feel their pastor is a brilliant man.

But I don't mean that we are stupid. Remember, the word "dumb" means "lacking the power of speech," or "temporarily speechless." And that is a description that fits us preachers real often.

I recall, for example, the funeral I conducted for George's third wife. George, who was 85, had held up well at the funeral home, but refused to return to his car after the simple ceremony at the grave.

Sensing that he might need me to offer him comfort, I quietly asked the undertaker to allow him to stay for awhile. Everyone departed but the two of us and George remained motionless, staring into the grave.

I remembered poignant scenes like this that I had seen in old movies, and wanted so much to be able to offer just the right words of consolation to George in this heart-rending moment.

Slowly I walked over to stand beside George, and gently put my arm around him. I remembered that sometimes it is best not to say anything, but just to be there.

George looked at me as though he expected a few words of wisdom, but I said nothing, feeling sure by now that just being there with him was sufficient. Then George broke the silence.

"Well, preacher," he said, in a strong voice, "I've planted three of 'em, and ain't a one of 'em come up yet."

Speechless, I walked to my car and drove home. There are moments when even a preacher knows it is time to quit.

The death of another woman provided a moment to remember. The mortician called and asked me to meet the family in his office. I had known the woman since she was a shut-in member of the church I was serving then, but I had never met any of her relatives.

The family members were two of her sons. Nervously the friendly undertaker said, "Pastor, the family did not want to have a funeral; they simply wanted me to bury their mother. But I insisted that they permit you to hold a simple graveside service."

I turned to the oldest son, and said I would be glad to help them in this way. He replied crisply, "Preacher, all we really want to do is put her in the ground. If we must have a funeral service, we want it to be short and sweet, with as few words as possible."

Once again I was dumbstruck! This was their mother he was talking about, as though she were but a sack of garbage to be buried.

Well, we didn't throw Momma from the trian, but we did bury her in record time, the shortest funeral I have ever conducted. Needless to say, I did not hang around after the benediction to console those two fellows.

What I heard about one preacher could have happened to me a dozen times over the years. I just thank God it hasn't — yet. It seems this pastor had a funeral on the first Saturday in December, during the Auburn-Alabama football game.

As he slowly led the procession toward the cemetery, he turned in the game on his car radio. Then he noticed up ahead on his right a shopping center, and remembered that his wife has asked him to bring home some milk. Auburn was on the two yard line, about to score.

Engrossed in the game, but thinking how proud his wife would be that he had not forgotten the milk, he turned into the parking lot of the shopping center. As he made the turn, Auburn scored, and he suddenly realized where he was, and why that long line of cars, with their headlights on, were following him — into the parking lot!

But even though preachers are often dumb, as he was then, they are also very resourceful. That pastor, though suddenly short of breath and sweating profusely, quickly turned his car toward the exit and watched in embarrassment as the long line of cars obediently followed him into the parking lot and back out onto the highway.

So, remember, even "dumb" preachers can lead people to the Lord. We just need to remember to not try doing it during the Auburn-Alabama game!

A Rustic Cabin In The Cumberland Mountains

When our four sons were growing up, we lived for awhile in Nashville, a city we loved and enjoyed. One weekend in April we packed a bag and took off for the hills, just wanting to get out of town for a night or two.

Without a reservation or any planning, we drove about 100 miles southeast of Nashville to a beautiful state park which had cabins for rent. We rented one with a fireplace and were soon happily gathered around a roaring fire while mom prepared ham sandwiches for supper.

I can close my eyes and still see that rustic cabin, that stone hearth, those big logs burning, and the smiles on our faces. If I had the money to build a place in the mountains, I would want it modeled after that cabin. We stayed but one night, and we have never been back, but it seems like just yesterday that we were there.

That night a gentle snow began to fall and to our joyful surprise by morning the ground was covered with God's lovely white blanket. I can still see the sun glistening through those snow-covered trees as we walked around, watching the boys romp and play. The snow was just right for making snowballs, and we threw a lot of them at each other on a magnificent day just made for fun.

The snow truly surprised us for spring was almost gome. The date was April 18, an easy day for us to remember since it was the anniversary of the birth of our first son. On that day years before the weather had not been at all pleasant where we lived, in Auburn on Lakeview Drive.

Dr. Ben Thomas had to drive through a torrential rain to get to Opelika, where he delivered David at what is now the East Alabama Medical Center. It was on that day in 1953 that a vicious tornado ripped through Lee County, destroying many homes and much property.

Now, in this secluded mountain hideaway, on another 18th of April, we remembered David, now dead, and the tornado, and the damage it had done to our rented home. We were thankful for the contrast: joy with our boys instead of the pain and anxiety of birth, and gentle snow in the place of fierce winds and rain.

For a few hours we were free from the cares of life, with no schedules to meet, no hectic sounds of busy city life, and hardly anyone else around to distract us. There was no buying and no selling, no horns being blown by impatient drivers, no yelping by the neighborhood dogs.

Many times since then my mind has gone back to that mini-vacation and the good feeling it gave our family. It was not expensive. It did not require a lot of travel. It was a simple setting, with no rides, or games, or cotton candy.

It was peaceful. We were relaxed. There was no family spat brewing, and the boys played together without the friction and arguments that sometimes spoiled our outings.

Can it be that my memory of that trip is so positive because it was such a pleasant experience? Or is it because of the inexpressible beauty of the location? I don't know. I do know that I often wish we could go back and enjoy that weekend again.

Since I cannot go back in time, I do hope I will not live so long that I forget that wonderful time in the Cumberland Mountains of Tennessee. On lazy days, when the rain is peppering down outside and my mind wanders back to the ineffable delight of those days when our boys were growing up, I wonder if they also remember some of those good times we shared.

I hope they do.

And I hope they feel like I do, that there are some things they would gladly do all over again.

Growing Old Is Not All Bad

Whatever lies ahead, I must confess that in my 60th year I am thoroughly enjoying living. From this perspective one can understand things that are impossible for the young and improbable for the very old.

Babies want their food. Children want their toys. Teenagers want their way. Young adults want everything now. Middle adults want to know why somebody didn't tell them how tough life was going to be.

The very old, unfortunately, often experience the diminishing of their mental faculties, until their fading grip on reality becomes no more than that of a child.

But folks my age, for a few years at least, have many advantages which come only with maturity. Not that we are "all wise," but we are able to see much of life in clearer perspective than we have ever seen it.

We see food not as infants do, as the primary need of life, but as something to savor and enjoy with friends. We do not live to eat. We see eating as one of many delightful necessities of life. By now we are more selective in choosing foods, avoiding some with good reason, and selecting others simply because we like them.

We are not as apt to care for toys as we once did. Shotguns, cars, and boats may have become toys for some of us, but by this time in life it has dawned on most of us that you can't find any comfort curling up at night with a shotgun or boat. None of our fancy gadgets can rub your back at night, or help you believe in yourself when life is falling apart. We value the love and respect of relatives and friends far more than toys and contraptions.

As for having our own way, we have learned by now that to insist on one's own way all the time is a good way to ruin one's life. Mature living involves give and take, being wrong sometimes, and understanding that none of us has a monopoly on wisdom. We are more likely to be understanding and forgiving now, while at age 20 we were often smart alecky and arrogant.

Having survived a few mid-life crises, we view others with a deeper appreciation. We know now how tough life can be. We have cried and hurt as many of our companions in former days became casualties instead of survivors. Friends will hear us say, "I am just glad to be alive and able to take nourishment!"

Folks in their 50s are able to look back to school days and shed a tear or two as they recall dear teachers who helped them grow up. Many times in recent years I have thought about my first grade teacher in Wetumpka. My heart overflows with gratitude when I remember Mrs. Oakley Melton. I think her first name was Dora. She was always just Mrs. Melton to me.

She came to mind again this fall when my grandson John started to school in Wetumpka. The first week he missed the bus one day and had a bad time until his parents came for him.

I still remember missing the bus one afternoon in the fall of 1938. I was frightened, started crying, and walked back into the school. I did not know what to do. Suddenly there was Mrs. Melton, reassuring me, and putting her arm around me. She got word to my parents, who lived 15 miles out in the country, that I would be at her home.

Then Mrs. Melton took me to her home not far away. Her chocolate fudge candy may have been the first I had ever eaten, and I know it was the best I have ever tasted. I played football in her front yard with her two sons until my mother arrived to take me home. One of her sons was Oakley, Jr. who became a fine attorney, like his father. The younger son, "Bimbo," later played football for the University of Alabama. Both of her sons were among my first heroes. Mrs. Melton was as good a woman as I have ever known. There just has to be a special place in heaven for saints like her, who give of themselves so unselfishly to help frightened children find their places in the world.

As I look back on experiences like that, I realize now that it was God who provided Mrs. Melton when I needed her. What seemed a dreadful experience turned out to be a blessing which I have remembered for more than 50 years. But it took all those years for me to see so clearly the hand of God at work in my life. I simply did not know then how good God really is.

It was Robert Browning who fashioned these lines:

Grow old along with me!
The best is yet to be,
The last of life, for which the first was made:
Our times are in his hand
Who saith "A whole I planned,
Youth shows but half; trust God: see all, nor
be afraid!"

I ponder these lines now and wonder: Perhaps the best is not, for my age, yet to be; it could be that the best of this earthly life is *at hand*, and we have but to realize that, and celebrate it!

That I choose to believe, so before my mental prowess fades into a second childhood, I intend to live as though these are the best years of my life. Maybe growing old is not so bad after all. It all depends on one's perspective.

The Simple Life Seems Gone Forever

The controversy over Auburn's drinking water is one of many indicators which reveals how complicated modern living has become. The simple life is apparently gone forever.

There was a time when a man could milk his cows in peace. If there was a city council in town, he probably did not know it existed, and even if he knew, the council was of no concern to him and his family.

Growing up in Elmore County, on a farm, I learned as a child how to milk cows. And it was customary for them to roam the pastures and the woods, especially during the fall and winter.

On our farm there were ponds and creeks which fed into the Tallapoosa River, and waste from our cows may have helped in a small way to cause the river water to look so brown and murky.

But back then the thought never entered my mind that cow manure washing into the creek may have contributed to the murkiness of the water. If anything, I must have had the childish notion that somehow the river was able to absorb such waste without it becoming a problem.

Years ago most of us thought nothing about swimming in creeks like Chewacla Creek, and the thought of pollution never came up. I can remember drinking cool water in the summertime from many springs on and around our farm. Now I would be rather reluctant to scoop up some water in my hands and have a drink from such a spring.

The water we drank from a family well was clean years ago or least we thought it was. Now we find that we need a dependable water filter system if we want to enjoy water that smells and tastes good.

Now what happens on a farm affects the people who live in town. In earlier years folks on the farms didn't think too much about what went on in town, except when we needed supplies, or when we went into town on Saturdays to enjoy popcorn and a picture show featuring Gene Autry or Roy Rogers.

Once a man could go into the woods and gather firewood for his family. Now we must protect our trees and try to find the funds to pay for expensive gas or electric heat.

As a boy I enjoyed listening to *The Lone Ranger* on the radio. Sometimes my friends or cousins and I had fun pretending to be The Lone Ranger and his sidekick, Tonto. We never imagined that we were insulting the Indians. We were just caught up in that wonderful "make believe" world of small children.

These days parents have to be careful about how they allow their kids to portray Tonto. Mr. Two Elk of the American Indian Movement can get outraged by the sight of white people waving tomahawks and acting like Indians. It makes one wonder what Indian children do for fun. Perhaps they play it safe by pretending to be Vikings or cavemen.

Schools are not simple anymore. The days of segregation are ended, which is one change, but there are many more differneces in the school house now. Buses are still yellow, but the kids on them are not just black and white any longer.

Amy, a teacher in our family, tells an interesting story of her first day teaching a junior high class in Montgomery. When she asked her students to stand and repeat together the pledge of allegiance to the flag, one boy remained seated in the back of the room.

Feeling that she had to demonstrate her authority, she insisted that the young fellow stand up, or, she said jokingly, "I will ship you off to Iran."

It turned out that the boy's name was Fawad, and his native country was, indeed, Iran, though at the time Amy assumed he was simply a stubborn, red-blooded American lad. Amy said her face remained red for hours!

The simple life of the past had its advantages. Farm boys had an edge on city slickers. We learned skills that kids in town never knew, like how to milk a cow.

When my speech professor at Auburn University asked his students to prepare a five-minute speech on a subject about which we were well-informed, I chose as my theme, "How to Milk a Cow."

It was as easy as falling off a log. I knew what I was talking about because I had milked so many cows. I could describe vividly the cow's tail, loaded with cockleburs, hitting me in the face as the cow tried in vain to drive flies away.

I was able to share how it felt to be almost finished milking and have the cow suddenly step in the bucket, or kick it over, so that I would have to return to the house and face my parents emptyhanded. They never seemed to be satisfied with my explanation that it was the cow's fault that I had no milk for the next meal.

It seems so unfortunate that my children and grandchildren are growing up so disadvantaged as to have never known the sting of cockleburs in a cow's tail on the cheek. But such are the deprivations of the complicated life in this modern world.

Though change is inevitable, I do hope that reminiscing never goes out of style. A few of us have got to preserve the stories of the simple life.

As nice as supermarkets are, it would be tragic for future generations not to know how grandma used to make jelly, preserve figs, can beans, and milk cows.

To Die Laughing Would Be A Great Way To Go

The Good Book says people are made in the image of God. That sounds rather spiritual or theological to some folks.

To me it is funny. And it's good news.

It is funny because it means that the great God of the universe is a being who in some way resembles us human beings. That is a truly hysterical thought: that the eternal God would copy us after himself!

It is good news because it means that God can laugh! When I think of all my sins, it is no small comfort to remember that God has a sense of humor.

Actually there is plenty of evidence in creation that God has a sense of humor. Only Someone with a delightful sense of humor would have made a skunk, or a parrot, or a giraffe. Such funny things could never have merely crawled out of the slime of some swamp.

Take the tiny gnat for example. Surely they serve no good purpose in the world. So God must have made them just for fun. God must crack up laughing at us who are so strong, yet so unable to prevent a gnat from flying up our noses. A lot of us long-winded preachers have swallowed more gnats than we would care to admit!

God's Son Jesus saw the humor in gnats. He poked fun at people who are so silly as to "strain out a gnat while swallowing a camel." Folks must have laughed out loud to have Jesus paint such a vivid picture of human foolishness.

The Bible really starts off in a somewhat humorous vein. If you don't laugh, you at least smile when Adam explains to God that eating the apple was not his fault. "It was the woman's fault," he says like a little child, "she gave the fruit to me."

Since Eve has no one to blame, she excuses herself by stammering that the serpent made her do it. What is funny is that from the beginning, every Adam and every Eve have taken turns blaming someone else for their sins.

Then there is the story of Noah. Forget how many days it rained. Just think about how Noah must have felt one day to discover that he was the only guy on earth who had received a message from heaven to build an ark.

The sun is shining and there are no dark clouds in the sky, and Noah hears God tell him to build this big ship on dry land. Can't you just hear him reply, "Sure, Lord, sure; build a gigantic boat right here on dry land in my back yard. Okay . . . ."

Then when he begins to obey God and build the ark, think about the time the poor man must have had explaining to his wife and children what he was doing.

"Yes, honey, a big boat, a very big boat, one that will hold a lot of animals," Noah says.

And Mrs. Noah stands there, with her hands on her hips, staring at him, saying, "A what? You have gone off the deep end this time for sure. I told you not to eat the berries off that strange-looking bush!"

Abraham and Sarah are a funny pair too. In fact the word "laugh" first appears in the Bible when Abraham received that shocking message from God that Sarah would have a baby at age 90. Abraham did what any old man would have done: he laughed out loud.

But he did more than laugh. He took Sarah downtown and bought her some maternity clothes, and waited expectantly until the promised son was born.

Abraham and Sarah thought it was so funny that they named their son "laughter." That's what the word Isaac means.

Ever since then, whenever a baby is born, you will find people standing around laughing. There is some crying too, but mostly babies make us laugh.

Jesus was no somber Savior who went around pronouncing judgment on people. One of the first places he took his disciples was to a party, the wedding feast at Cana.

It was at this party that Jesus turned 120 gallons of water into wine, so the party could go on. Our Lord was no sourpuss.

Ever since Jesus first turned water into wine, folks have been laughing about it. Remember the fellow who got stopped by the police with several gallons of moonshine in his car? He explained to the officer that there was only water in the jugs.

When the officer tasted some of it, and affirmed that it was indeed whiskey, the man exclaimed, "Well, what do you know; the Lord has done it again!"

Human beings are made so that we can become so tickled by some things that we think if we don't stop we may die laughing. Considering that the One who made us must have such a rich sense of humor, that might not be a bad way to go.

If I must choose, I would bet that when we exit this world, at least a few of us will find the good Lord laughing instead of frowning. After all, He knows that the next chapter for his kids is going to be a whole lot more fun than this earthly one.

If you still find it hard to believe that God has a sense of humor, go look in the mirror. Just look at what you see, and surely you will admit that God must have been laughing when he designed that funny face of yours.

Just be careful not to look in the mirror too long. You may die laughing.

Empty Is A Sad Word And A Dreadful Condition

Whenever my wife and I drive down Interstate 65 south of Montgomery, we always look for a dilapidated old house out in a pasture, a quarter of a mile from the highway. One of us will say, "There's our house."

Truth is we don't know anything about that wooden shack except that it has been empty for years. But for some strange reason I guess we adopted the house. Since the last time Dean remarked, "There's our house," I have wondered why we adopted it.

There is a chinaberry tree growing beside it, and we've heard the old saying that a chinaberry tree will bring good luck. But that is not the reason we call it our house.

Perhaps it's because it looks like a good place for a home. It is surrounded by good pasture land, and the nearby woods would be a wonderful place to walk and listen to squirrels and birds in the fall of the year. And there is a creek to the south which appers to have a good stream of water year-round. We have always loved walking in the bed of a shallow stream and looking for interesting rocks and Indian relics.

Then maybe we adopted that old house because it is located in Alabama not far from where we were born. We have been around the world and seen many beautiful places. We have wondered what it would be like to live in Hawaii, or England, or Costa Rica. But somehow we have always been drawn back to the land of our roots. We grew up playing in Alabama's clay and I guess that is as good a place as any finally to be laid to rest, back in the soil of our birth.

I have not asked Dean why we call it our house. But I think I know what she would say, and that would be my reason also. We have called it ours because it's empty, and it looks like it needs somebody. Other folks probably share with us this yearning to fill an old, empty house and turn it into a home.

Maybe the need to fill empty things is just part of what it means to be a human being.

Had she made a career of it, Dean would have been a first-rate interior designer. She is gifted with a delightful imagination, a gift she has used over and over again to turn an ordinary house into a charming home. I have seen her pick wild flowers out of a ditch and create for our dining room table a centerpiece that would make any florist envious.

With that same gift she has often come up with a delicious meal when, it seemed to me, there was nothing in the cupboard. I have told her many times that she reminds me of God, for like him, she has a knack for making something out of nothing. A man is mighty fortunate if he is married to a woman who has mastered the art of knowing how to "make do" when things are scarce.

An empty house, especially an old one, has a certain magnetism about it. It seems to be saying to all who pass by, "I'm lonely and I need somebody." We all know that an empty house seems to deteriorate faster than one with someone living in it.

The very word "empty" is a sad word, a word we use to describe many different things. We use it to paint a dreadful picture of depressing conditions.

When we are bored and idle, uninvolved in the ordinary demands of life, we may say the hours are empty. We mean that time is moving ever so slowly, and affording us no stimulation or joy. Hours drag on and on when life is destitute of meaning.

When we have forgotten or neglected to bring a dish of food or a gift, we may say to family or friends that we regret having arrived emptyhanded. Or we may go home from a party where others won prizes and we are sad because we returned emptyhanded.

Any of us would be embarrassed to have someone call us "emptyheaded," though we sometimes inflict that judgment upon our scatterbrained friends. Even in jest, with some truth in it, it is still no compliment and no word we want to be used about ourselves.

When death invades our ranks we often find ourselves facing an empty chair where once sat a dear loved one. Tears flow quickly when we remember that a chair now vacant was once a precious loved one's favorite chair. I once visited a man who showed me his wife's bedroom where, on a chair, a sweater was draped.

He said sadly, "I have kept her room exactly like she left it." She had been dead 20 years. That's sad. My friend had not only a bedroom that was empty because of his wife's death, he had an empty heart that was devoid of joy.

One of the cruelest jokes I have ever heard was about a Christmas gift given to a boy who was mentally handicapped. Some fellows in the neighborhood gave him the gift, wanting to have some fun at the poor boy's expense. When he opened it on Christmas morning, there was nothing in the box. It was empty, but not as empty as the hearts of the boys who wrapped the box. They were empty of pity and common decency.

Then there is the sadness of empty promises. It hurts to look back and remember how many times I disappointed my boys with empty promises. There were so many occasions when I foolishly canceled a fishing trip or a family outing because of the pressure of church business.

The boys are all grown and married now, but sometimes when they are home we are all reminded of those days when the family was "second" to whatever church duties called. Not long ago, as we sat down together for lunch, the telephone rang and I was away from the table for several minutes. When I returned, one of the boys got up without saying a word, and took the phone off the hook. He did it with authority and firmness.

I think he was saying something like this, "Dad, now that I am grown, I am big enough and smart enough to do with that telephone what you should have done more often when we were young." The irony of it all is that many times I neglected my family in order to prepare a sermon in which I admonished people to give their children plenty of "prime" time and not let their work become a god to them!

An empty house is a vacant house with no occupants. A house that is vacant does not sell as easily as one that is occupied. If we could assign human feelings to a vacant house, we might speak of it as a melancholy home, a place that appears doleful, mournful and gloomy. Those words paint a miserable picture, a condition that is not desirable for a home or a person.

A house needs voices, laughter, the sounds of children playing, the smell of food cooking, and that special "touch" of someone who knows how to make the place feel comfortable. The feeling that inspires us all to say from time to time, "There is just no place like home."

I suppose one day we will look out across that pasture south of Montgomery and discover that the old shack is no more, gone with the wind of changing times. If I could just win the Reader's Digest Sweepstakes . . . .

But if I had $10 million today, I am sure I would be broke within a month. Dean and I would buy all the old houses around town and spend everything trying to restore them.

But the first one we would buy would be that sad old house of ours on Interstate 65. It needs a friend.

Why Playing With Toys Is Not Simply Child's Play

Sometimes when people ask me where I grew up, I have a little fun with them. It's usually good for a laugh the way I describe the location of my dad's farm.

This is my response: "I grew up in Elmore County, south of Red Land, off the Rifle Range Road, down near Bingham Bend, about a mile from the Tallapoosa River."

I tried that answer recently on J. C. and Foy Ward, and they did not laugh. They knew the exact location I was talking about! To my amazement, Foy said, "I know where that land is because years ago my father rented and farmed that land."

Foy, who was recovering from surgery, even knew about my Uncle Dave's home. My folks took me there often when I was a child, and I loved his home. It was a big, beautiful country home, not far from my home, but up toward Red Land.

There were few paved roads out in the country when I was a boy. So it was often quite an adventure to see if Dad's old Ford could make it up the steep hills.

The slippery red clay of Elmore County made a good road bed when it was dry, but a few days of rain could turn those narrow county roads into a treacherous pathway. Many times the car would stall as the tires spun needlessly and the car would slowly slide sideways toward a ditch.

I am sure it was more fun to me as a child than it was to my father. While my sisters and I played in the mud, and Mom complained about the mess we were making of ourselves, my Dad had to walk to a neighbor's place in search of a tractor or some mules to pull the car out of the mire. Such childhood experiences, while exciting to me, were not much fun to Dad.

But it was always fun to visit Uncle Dave and Aunt Pearl. Their home was a two-story house with a magnificent winding stairway. I was fascinated with the stairs, since there were none in our home, and I loved to sneak a trip down the banisters when none of the adults was looking.

Uncle Dave loved children. He always had a couple of mechanical toys hidden in his desk. He liked to surprise us by letting us look at them while they performed. I can still hear him laughing as we watched with the amazement of children a little clown or some other toy dancing around on his coffee table. My favorite was the monkey that walked about in a circle while beating on a drum.

We were not allowed to touch the toys. When Uncle Dave felt we had enjoyed them enough, he would put them back into the safe haven of his great oak desk. This was his way of insuring that the toys would be available for the next child's visit.

I did not understand as a child why I was not allowed to play with the toys. Now I understand. Immitating Uncle Dave, I have bought a number of toys to use in amusing my grandchildren. My favorite was a Santa Claus for which I paid five dollars.

Only Santa cannot enjoy his battery-powered walk any more. One of my grandsons broke off one of his feet, so all Santa can do now is ring his little bell as his arms go back and forth. I should have been as wise as Uncle Dave and kept old Santa out of the range of those little rascals. It seems they not only enjoy seeing a toy move, they also enjoy fixing it so it cannot move.

When I was a boy our farm was always in danger of flooding when the Tallapoosa was swollen by spring rains. On one such occasion we moved up hill to safety and spent the night with Uncle Dave. That was exciting.

I can remember only one other time when we stayed overnight with Uncle Dave. Dad was serving on a jury for a man accused of murder. When the judge sequestered the jury one night, Mom took us up to Dave's. I still recall how worried we were about Dad, for we heard that the man on trial had threatened to kill the jurors if they found him guilty. He was convicted and sentenced to life in prison. Funny, I am not sure, but I think his name was Green.

Not many years ago Uncle Dave's wondrous old home burned to the ground. It was a strange feeling to drive by and view the smoldering ashes of a home which held so many memories for me. I wondered if his toys, still hidden perhaps, had perished in the flames.

How delightful it would have been to take my grandchildren to visit Uncle Dave's place. What stories I could tell them about his toys and my exciting trips down that banister!

But Uncle Dave is gone, and his old house is gone. They are only memories now, fading memories of a childhood that often seems a hundred years ago.

Still I am here, and there are children aplenty. If I am willing I can take the time to surprise them with a toy and create a sparkle in their eyes like my Uncle Dave did for me. It will require that I step down from being a stuffy old adult for a few minutes now and then, and try to see the world through a child's big eyes. It sounds like it might even be fun.

I wonder where I could find a toy monkey that beats a drum when it's wound up. Or a new foot for Santa Claus. If I keep thinking about Uncle Dave, I may get wound up myself.

Embarrassing Moments Add Excitement To Life

Moments of embarrassment come to us all, reminding us of our humanity. None of us is excluded, and preachers may be among the most vulnerable.

When a certain pastor's daughter returned home at three o'clock in the morning from a dance, her father greeted her very sternly.

"Good morning, child of the devil," he said grimly.

Respectfully and demurely, she replied, "Good morning, father."

That preacher was embarrassed by what he said. But one can also be embarrassed by what one is unable to say when the lights go out.

In my early days I used a manuscript when preaching. One Sunday evening a thunder storm erupted while I was delivering my sermon. The electricity was suddenly cut off, leaving the sanctuary in darkness except for the flashing of lightning.

Unable to see I stood helpless at the pulpit. Some of our ushers quickly lit some candles on the altar. The light, however, was too feeble for me to see clearly enough to read my sermon. Sheepishly, and red-faced, I admitted that our service would be concluded with prayer which, thank God, I was able to offer extemporaneously.

How embarrassing! To have to admit that I was unable to speak intelligently about the faith in the dark really caused me great pain. I vowed never to allow that to happen again. I went home that night so humiliated that I wanted to die. Speechless because the lights went out!

That experience, along with the persistent hounding of my wife, persuaded me to learn to preach without notes. In those years she was relentless in reminding me that preaching was simply not convincing unless it was done with eye contact and without notes.

She would not even permit me a single 3 x 5 card. At first I thought she was unfair and unreasonable. Now I realize that her demand for excellence was like the irritating grain of sand in the oyster, causing me to develop a skill I thought might never be mine.

I still remember the first time I ever went into the pulpit without a single note. It was exhilarating! Comparable to the feeling one must have in jumping out of an airplane with a parachute for the first time.

Embarrassment can thus become a catalyst for change in our lives. It can cause us to become better prepared for our responsibilities in the future.

Preaching without notes does present certain dangers to the preacher. One has a tendency to ramble on and on, and sometimes to forget a point or a story that was in the prepared manuscript. Fortunately no one realizes something was forgotten and few people these days ever wish a sermon had been longer.

I have concluded more than once that God may have extended his mercy to my congregation by causing me to forget some story or poem that I had intended to use.

Even on those rare Sundays when the sermon may have been a sizzler, I have never had a line of folks waiting to complain that the sermon was not long enough. As much as people may love good preaching, few of them seem to like it very much after noon.

That fact may explain why one man said, "Preacher, no matter how good your sermon, nobody hears what you say after twelve o'clock."

The famed missionary, Albert Schweitzer, once visited the United States, raising money for his work in Africa. Following an evening lecture at Aspen, Colorado, reporters pressed him to explain what he meant by "reverence for life."

"All right, gentlemen," Schweitzer said, "I will give you one more illustration of what I mean. As of this minute, we are going to start reverencing my life. You are going home, and I am going to bed!"

It has been said that the great evangelist George Whitfield could pronounce the word "Mesopotamia" in such a way as to reduce his audience to tears. That may be true, but I imagine most of our parishioners today would rather have a preacher who knows when to pronounce the benediction.

That bit of kindness expresses a much desired "reverence" for that part of their anatomies which must endure that strange structure we call the church pew. The pain to the end can only be endured, folks tell me, if the end of the sermon is in sight.

Eagles push their young out of the nest, forcing them to learn to fly. That seems a bit heartless, but it is nothing compared to what parents do to their children so that the kids can learn to live in the real world.

The womb is a warm, safe haven. Babies like it so much that they scream in protest when their mothers finally force them to enter this noisy, crazy world on their own.

No wonder babies yell. When they finally make their way through that narrow tunnel, someone gives them a whack on the behind, and cuts their life line. What a rude way to become acquainted with larger human beings.

Then before long mom and dad will take the little darling to church and deposit it in something called a nursery. Before Junior can even talk or walk, he has to learn to cope with a perfect stranger who is silently praying that the little rascal will keep his mouth shut until the church service has ended.

During these nursery days the little fellow surely has no idea why he is being moved around. The baby bed looks a lot like the one at home and that bottled juice still tastes like the same old stuff. About the only thing that may be different is that on the wall of the nursery he may see a picture of some strange looking man with a beard, dressed in a bathrobe, and holding a cute little animal in his arms.

He hears someone call those little animals "lambs." But about the time he thinks he has this figured out, some nice lady calls him a "sweet little lamb." Not only is he confused, but he thinks to himself, "My Lord, do I really look like that strange thing the guy with the beard is holding in his arms?"

Nursery days fly by and the kid adapts to his home. He learns to walk, to climb, to explore, and he discovers that he can do things which absolutely delight his parents. He smiles, sheepishly but proudly, when dad proclaims one day, "At last

Junior is potty-trained!" He cannot remember when his parents seemed happier.

So five or six years pass and the little boy begins to feel secure, almost as comfortable as he was in the womb. He can speak and communicate. He can feed himself. He has a wonderful sense of being somebody. He understands big words like family, toilet, mistake, and spanking.

But about the time he begins to enjoy home and family, his parents burst his bubble. They get him up at dawn every morning, make him eat whether he is hungry or not, and tell him he has to start riding that giant yellow machine called a bus. As if that's not bad enough, he discovers that he has to ride in that yellow thing with a hundred other kids, some of whom are screaming all the time for no apparent reason.

This new jolt to his nervous system, he learns, is called going to school. Nobody explains why he must go. He gets no sympathy from his parents. He is lucky, they tell him, for they had to walk barefooted to school, through snow storms while fighting off wild bears with a stick.

Suddenly little Junior is thrust into a classroom with 35 other frightened kids, and his heart begins to pound. There at the front of the room is a giant person called a teacher. For some strange reason the teacher does not know any of the kids, and starts asking each one to stand up and say his name.

Talk about being pushed out of the nest! Junior is so flooded with self-consciousness that he turns bright red, sure that all the other kids will laugh at the way he says his name. His days of laughing about the Cookie Monster in the safety of his home are over. Now he is face to face with that ugly beast who scares the daylight out of every human being: the terrible Stage Fright Monster.

Junior finds that it gets worse. The teacher acquaints him with grades so for the first time in his life he learns what it means to fail or succeed. This is frightening enough, but he discovers also that whether he fails or not will depend a lot on his ability to remember things.

He learns that his ability to memorize information is stimulated by competition with the other kids and by his own desire to succeed. Quickly he recognizes this burning in his chest to be a winner, not a loser. So even though he has not chosen to go to school, he is at this very young age suddenly threshing about in the stream of the American educational system.

I can identify with little Junior, for in 1938 I was little Walter Junior in that first grade class. I can remember being scared to death that a giant teacher expected me to memorize a long thing called a poem. Impossible, I thought. But as I saw other kids memorizing poetry, I began to believe that I could.

Even so I had no way of knowing what a dreadful feeling of nervousness would come upon me when I stood up before others to recite a poem. Heavens, it was awful! It was not just my knees that shook, I was trembling all over.

Back then some schools taught both poetry and prose in a class known as "Expression." I can still remember sweating long hours, with mamma standing over me like a tyrant, pushing me to learn to read well and to recite the poems assigned to me. It would be years later before I had any appreciation for mamma's relentless pressure.

About the time I was adjusting fairly well to the disciplines of expression, mamma really threw me a curve by insisting that I take voice lessons. I could not believe it. Why me? My dad could not sing at all. He could call cows from five miles away, but he could not carry a tune in a bucket. And now I, his son, was expected to learn to sing!

Once again the Stage Fright Monster was breathing down my neck. It was one thing to stand up and recite a poem or read a story, but walk out and sing a song from memory — that was insane!

But like the eagle pushing her eaglet out of the nest, parents seem not to hear the silent screams of their young. "You can do it, son, I know you can if you will just try," they say without mercy.

So stage fright or not, I was soon studying voice under the expert guidance of a beautiful blind singer, Florence Golson Bateman. It was she who taught me how to breathe, using the diaphragm so that air is available when it is needed.

I found it was fun, not only to sing, but to think that you could. Soon I was singing "Ole Man River," "Invictus," "On the Road to Mandelay," and others. The strangest one, to me at least, was one about "Who Is Sylvia?" I would still like to find out who Sylvia was before I die.

Singing songs in the home of a lovely, sympathetic teacher is one thing. But when Mrs. Bateman told me there would be a "recital" in the school auditorium, I almost fainted! I could not believe she wanted me to stand up and sing all by myself before an audience. At that moment I knew how the little eaglet feels when he has been pushed out of the nest. Horrified!

To my surprise I lived through those recitals. Perhaps I survived them because at the last moment before it was my turn to step out on the stage, I went into some kind of merciful coma. Afterward I could hardly remember having sung. In fact, my friends told me that in one recital I walked out nonchalantly and yawned before I sang.

I did not believe them at first. Later I learned that yawning is just another sign of nervousness, like giggling or crying. Nonchalant? No, sir, buddy, I was pertrified.

My wife remembers a frightening moment when she performed in a piano recital. Edna Earl, who preceded her on the stage, forgot her music, started over several times, and finally quit in embarrassment.

Dean remembers turning to Blanton and saying, "I'm not afraid, are you?" Whereupon their teacher spoke sharply to her, saying, "Don't say that word in here; don't dare say that word again!" And without taking a breath, she sent Dean out onto the stage to perform. She did well but also could not remember much about it later. Another coma perhaps.

And so it goes. All through life old Stage Fright stalks us all, no matter what our age. We may outgrow our childish imaginations of monsters lurking in every dark place, but few of us ever reach the point that we are completely free of the influence of the Stage Fright Monster. He tortures us to the grave.

Teachers and parents try relentlessly to help us discover who we are, so that we can become comfortable with ourselves. But we are afraid, fearful we will fail or be embarrassed. When fear engulfs us, then old Stage Fright laughs, for he has won again.

As we grow older we do find that occasionally we can whip old Stage Fright and not allow him to spoil our best efforts by succumbing to knee-knocking, heart-pounding nervousness. And if once, perhaps we can wrestle him down again and again.

After all, as terrified as the eaglet must be when first pushed overboard, the little tyke does learn to fly, and by flying becomes eventually a big eagle. So, too, Junior must learn to leave the nest and wrestle with old Stage Fright if he would soar to the heights of magnificent living.

Mom and Dad just need to remember that little junior never learns any of this until he has wrestled with old Stage Fright for years. So push him out as gently as you can.

All The Fun Not Reserved For Youth

Under normal conditions it is fun to be a child. Children can dress up like witches and ghosts, eat too much candy, and play make believe games until they are exhausted.

The lucky ones are then tucked into a warm bed by loving parents who give them a kiss and gratefully commit them to the Lord while they sleep. They can slip peacefully into the land of nod without any worry at all about increased taxes, overdrawn checks, or a late car payment.

The next day the kids can plan a pajama party, play with the dog, and dream of one day getting the winning hit in the World Series. They can play with dolls, plan a trip to the mall on Saturday, admire a collection of baseball cards, and make a thousand wishes upon a star.

The teen years can also be packed with fun, especially if mom and dad are still paying most of the bills. Teenagers can really burn rubber on the streets if dad paid for the tires.

They can stay out until dawn on Friday nights, then complain to high heaven if mom wakes them up before noon. "Rake the lawn? Are you kidding? I did that last year! Get off my back, mom!"

Teenagers are apt to think that money grows on trees, and that no matter what the costs, they have got to have the same designer jeans and shoes that the other kids are wearing. Parents simply must bow down and worship at the altar of the peer pressure god.

Young people are beginning to be aware of many of the problems of adulthood, but they are also getting smarter by the day. By the time they are 16, they are so much wiser than their parents that they are certain that if their parents were not so dumb, everything would be fine.

But in spite of all the "growing pains" parents experience while their kids are growing up, most parents do want their teenagers to have lots of fun. They are apt to make sacrifices in order that their kids may enjoy privileges which their parents were denied. As dumb as parents are, they realize that there is plenty of time later for teenagers to worry about mortgages and mammograms.

But all the fun in life is not reserved for the young. It is just packaged differently in the adult years, and adults have to look harder for it. Fun for the middle-aged is more often found in simple things.

Recently, for example, I had a marvelous time watching Auburn lose a football game, in the company of two of my sons and two of my grandsons. Not that I enjoyed watching the Tigers lose, for I am a diehard Auburn fan.

But somewhere during the third quarter my oldest son Matt turned to me and said, "This is fun, Dad; this is the first time we have ever been to an Auburn game together. We need to do this again." I agreed, as a warm feeling spread all over me.

There we were with his two sons, 14 and 11, and it dawned on him that it was fun for us to be together. And what a thrill it was to hear him express that thought!

I wondered out loud if he was right, and we decided he was. When he was growing up, I sat in the stands watching him, and his brothers, play many football games. We had even been to a couple of Senior Bowl games together. But we had never sat together watching Auburn, my alma mater, play a game.

When an Auburn player recovered a fumble, we rehashed the most memorable moment of his high school football days. The Demopolis Tigers were playing Clanton in the district playoffs. Matt was a starting linebacker.

Matt's moment of glory came late in the game when the Clanton quarterback fumbled the ball in his own end zone. Matt pounced on the loose ball for a touchdown, and that score provided the margin of victory for Demopolis.

"My one day of glory,"Matt said, laughing.

I remembered how proud I had been that night, so proud that I let everybody around me in the stands know that it was "my boy" who had recovered that fumble. Matt smiled as I told him about that.

Years from now I will not remember what team beat Auburn on that recent Saturday. But I will remember my grown son telling me how much fun it was for us to be together at the game.

The icing on that cake came as we were walking out of the stadium. Matt's youngest son, Garrett, said, "Thanks for taking us to the game, Granddaddy; this is the first time I have ever been to an Auburn game."

Garrett was beaming all over, but not any more than I was.

Garrett was a child having fun, but I knew that he has had a lot of heartache also. His parents were divorced when he was very young, and Matt is his stepfather. It has not been easy to get adjusted to a "new dad" in the home. That is hard on a child, any child.

However, this summer Garrett's mom told me about a beautiful conversation she had with her boys recently. After six years of living together, Mike asked Matt, "Would you mind if I called you 'Dad' when other kids are around? It will save having to explain a lot of things." Matt naturally agreed.

Tammy glowed with joy when she told me that one night Garrett said to her, "Mom, I guess you have made a lot of mistakes, but you didn't make a mistake when you married Matt. He makes a pretty good Dad."

No, all the fun in life is not reserved for the kids. Grandparents can have fun too, lots of it. You just have to look for it in the right places.

By the way, does anyone know where I can get six tickets to the next Auburn game?

Reflections On The Life Of A Good Friend

We buried my friend Stanhope Brasfield last week. I will miss him, and I will never forget him.

He was one tough man: a man's man. So it was no surprise to see so many men turn out for his funeral. The church was packed, and many stood along the back wall.

Known for his wit, Stanhope must have loved seeing such a big crowd. He always beamed proudly when there was a big crowd for church. If he could have talked to us, he would have probably said, "I never knew I had this many friends, but where were they when I needed them!"

He did have a lot of friends because he was a friend to many. Those who knew him would say that he was one of those rare men "whose word was his bond." If he told you something, you could count on it.

Stanhope raised a family on a farm just south of Demopolis, just off Highway 43 that goes on to Linden, the county seat of Marengo County. He built up the land, lived off the land, raised cattle and chickens, and grew vegetables.

I sat at his table for meals many times. When we went for lunch, he would always say, "We eat at 12:15; don't be late." He was busy and disciplined; there were things to do, and there wasn't time for "just fooling around."

I said he was tough. He was. But it was more than a physical toughness. He was mentally tough, emotionally tough, and morally tough. His arms were bronzed by years of working hard out in the sunshine, but there was something winsome about him which went beyond his physical appearance.

His speech, his alertness, his keen mind, his caring spirit, his reverence for life — all these qualities made one constantly aware that this was a man of character, someone of genuine integrity. He was more than a man, more than a farmer; he was a man in whom the image of God was reflected, and that contagiously. You found yourself wanting to be like him.

But if he was tough, he was also gentle. He loved to carve wooden toys for children, and especially for his own grandchildren. He enjoyed making crosses, and many of his friends are proud to own an attractive little wooden cross which Stanhope made.

Stanhope was not reluctant to talk about his faith but he left the teaching to his wife, Laura. For years she taught the couples Sunday school class which they both loved. This class developed a fellowship which has been treasured by all who shared in it.

When his beautiful wife, a brilliant teacher and devoted Christian, became ill with Alzheimer's disease, Stanhope's faith was shaken but not destroyed. In fact his faith became stronger.

His influence became stronger too. There came from Stanhope no screams of self-pity, but instead a courageous resolve to keep Laura at home and to care for her himself.

He asked the Lord to allow him to live long enough to care for his wife as long as she lived. So for some eight years God granted his wish. Most of that time Laura did not know anyone, even her husband, but Stanhope refused to believe that her mind was gone. He took her riding, talked to her, fed her, and cared for her — even though she was unable to respond in any way.

I saw her in that condition not long before she died. It broke my heart, and Stanhope and I were in tears, unable to speak as I left their home that day. But I drove away knowing that I had been in the presence of a real man that day.

When I was his pastor Stanhope was my friend and faithful co-worker in the church. But his friendship was not shallow; it was tough, tough enough that he would tell me the truth when he felt I needed to hear it. That he did more than once, for pastors need correction like everyone else does.

I can close my eyes and see him, sitting in my study. He would come by in his work clothes, and tell me in plain English about something I was neglecting or overlooking. He would tell me that I needed to take care of it, and that he knew that I would. He never stayed long; he got to the point and went on about his business.

Whenever he had left me, I would sit there with tears in my eyes, thanking God for this rare man. I knew that he had told me the truth, and I knew that he loved me. And I knew that I would be a fool not to follow his advice!

When he learned from his doctor that he would soon die from cancer, Stanhope called me. He said he wanted me to come over before long and help with his funeral. I promised him I would.

A few weeks later I drove over to see him and we talked about dying and about his funeral. He was ready to go, and had no complaints against God. He still refused to feel sorry for himself and insisted on telling me how good God had been to him.

The concerns he expressed were not for himself, but for his children and grandchildren. He wanted them, each one, of whom he was so very proud, to know God, and to love God. If they follow his example, they will.

I asked him what he wanted me to say at his funral. He dodged the question by saying, "You know what to do." Then he paused and laughed as he said, "I don't want no mess!" I laughed because I knew what he meant.

He meant that he did not want me to get up in the pulpit and mouth off a lot of sentimental platitudes; he wanted me to tell the truth. He did not want folks who listened to my eulogy to wonder if that was really Stanhope in that casket.

I did my best to honor his request. I told the truth, but it dawned on me as I planned my remarks — Stanhope had not needed to give me a message which I could share at his funeral. The man himself, the life he lived, that was the message. His life was his message. And it spoke with more clarity than any words a preacher could utter.

Speaking of words, Stanhope had a lot of colorful phrases he used to describe folks. When the church was raising money for some project, I asked him about a certain man. He replied tersely, "You won't have any luck fishing up that creek; that man is as close as the bark on a tree." I found out he was right. He usually was.

Some folks will pray for you but never manage to do much more than pray for you. That was not Stanhope. I recall one cold winter night, when my wife was sick, that Stanhope came to the house, not for a visit but to bring us some meat, potatoes, cornbread, and turnip greens. Such a man is impossible to forget.

Stanhope Brasfield — a man. But more than a man. He was God's man.

The world is a better place because Stanhope lived in it for awhile. And I am a better man for having been his friend.